Gay Men
Choosing
Parenthood

Gay Men

Choosing

Parenthood

Gerald P. Mallon

Columbia University Press   New York

Columbia University Press
Publishers Since 1893
New York   Chichester, West Sussex

© 2004 Columbia University Press
All rights reserved

Library of Congress Cataloging-in-Publication Data
Mallon, Gerald P.
   Gay men choosing parenthood / Gerald P. Mallon.
   p. cm.
   Includes bibliographical references and index.
   ISBN 0–231–11796–5 (cloth : alk. paper) — ISBN
   0–231–11797–3 (pbk. : alk. paper)
   1. Gay fathers—United States—Interviews. 2. Gay
   fathers—United States—Psychology. 3. Gay fathers—
   United States—Attitudes. 4. Gay adoption—United
   States. 5. Fatherhood—United States—Psychological
   aspects. I. Title.

   HQ76.2.USM313 2004
   306.874'2—dc21
                                            2003055086

Columbia University Press books are printed on
permanent and durable acid-free paper.

Printed in the United States of America

c 10 9 8 7 6 5 4 3 2 1
p 10 9 8 7 6 5 4 3 2 1

For Mike Rendino

Contents

Acknowledgments ix

Prologue xi

Introduction: Gay and Lesbian
Parenting—an Overview   I

1. The Journey Toward Parenting   23

2. Creating Family   59

3. Community Responses to Gay Dads   107

4. Gender Politics and Gay Male
Parenthood   131

Appendix: Field Experience
in Retrospect   149

References 159

Index 171

About the Author 177

Acknowledgments

Nine years ago, my life changed dramatically in the hallway of a large gothic church in New York City. I was attending a friend's commitment ceremony and saw another guest standing in the hallway with a five-year-old holding his hand and a toddler clinging to his leg. Both children were so obviously in love with this man, their daddy, that anyone could tell that they were a family. Trying to be sardonically witty, I approached them and said, "These aren't your children, are they?" His eyes flashed with anger. "Yes, of course, they're my children!" It was too late to say that I was only joking, but I said embarrassedly, "It's obvious," and quickly walked away, castigating myself for the clumsy attempt to initiate a conversation with this very attractive man. During the ceremony, while I was trying to shake off the bad feeling of the interaction, I realized that I was still intrigued by this man and his children. I realized that I was attracted not only to him but to the obvious connection he had with his children. With some surprise I realized how desperately I wanted that kind of connection in my life.

During the reception I took a deep breath and approached the man and his kids again and started the conversation with more grace. Mike and I started talking, and I was introduced to his two sons. Not long after, we fell in love. Nine years later I still marvel at my great luck in meeting Mike. He and the boys may never really understand my gratitude to them for embracing me in their lives and making me part of their family. I don't think that they will ever know how desperately I wanted to be a parent and how I believed that I never would have that opportunity as a gay man. I am thankful every single day for their support and for their love, despite my imperfections.

For all these years I've had the privilege of watching Mike's absolute dedication to being a parent. He is the kind of father that all children wish they could have. He's the kind of father I wish for every child I ever worked with in foster care. His unconditional love for his children is matched by the astonishing energy, enthusiasm, and vitality with which he approaches parenthood day after day. I have never met a man who has been a more magnificent father to his children. His compassion and commitment to parenting cause me to have the most profound respect and admiration for him as a person, a parent, and as my partner. It is an honor to dedicate this book to him.

I am grateful also to the gay dads who permitted me to interview them for this book and who trusted me with their personal stories. I am grateful too to Terry Boggis, the director of Center Kids at the Lesbian, Gay, Bisexual, and Trangender Center in New York, and to Dr. April Martin, the author of the finest book about lesbian and gay parenting, for inspiring me throughout the process of writing this book and for so generously sharing with me their vast knowledge of lesbian and gay parents.

I would also like to thank my colleagues at the Hunter College School of Social Work and the National Resource Center for Foster Care and Permanency Planning, who have been a source of inspiration for me and provided me with a solid home base from which to work. I am proud to be associated with such a wonderful school.

My thanks also to John Michel, senior editor at Columbia University Press, with whom I have worked on three books and, I hope, more to follow. John is a pleasure to work with and has been patient with my many delays in writing this book.

And, finally, I want to thank to my good friend and colleague Laura Markowitz, editor of *In the Family* magazine, for her remarkable abilities as an editor and for being such a creative spirit in my life. Laura always makes what I write sound better because her gentle handling of my words adds a healthy portion of love to them.

Prologue

I have always loved children, and there has always been a part of me that wanted to be a dad. As a gay man, I thought it was impossible—who was gonna let me be someone's parent? And it wasn't like I could just go out and get pregnant myself and have a baby. I guess I had internalized a lot of the homophobia that I had been fed somewhere along the way: I believed that gay people could not be good parents, just because they were gay. It made me sad. I was always close to my sister's kids, but it wasn't enough to be the really devoted uncle; I wanted to be something more for a child. One day I thought, Why not? Why can't I be a dad?' I could be a great dad for some child. I had a lot of the qualities that make for a great parent. And so I set out to become someone's dad. Five years ago I adopted Peter, and I have never been the same since.

For the last two decades a quiet revolution has been blooming in the gay male community. More and more gay men from all walks of life are becoming parents. Gay men have had to be creative and overcome many obstacles to become parents. Aside from those who had children in previous, heterosexual, unions, gay men who chose parenthood after coming out may have contracted with a surrogate mother to bear their children. Some may have become donor dads, donating their sperm to lesbian friends and then entering into complex coparenting agreements with them. Others managed to navigate the heterocentric adoption and foster care systems and became parents that way. But no matter what their method was, these gay dads share similar experiences. *Gay Men Choosing Parenthood* explores the lives of twenty gay men who had become fathers by choice in the 1980s and had done so outside the boundaries of a heterosexual union. In writing this book, I wanted in particular to find out how and why these gay men chose to become fathers and to explore the changes in their lives at work, in the gay community, and in their neighborhood communities as a result of their decision to become parents. After interviewing twenty pioneers in the gay fatherhood movement, I have come to believe that their experiences necessitate new definitions of fatherhood. *Gay Men Choosing Parenthood* is the first of what I hope will be many efforts in the gay community to describe and explore how gay fathers are changing society as a whole, and for the better.

This is a far different book from what I originally envisioned. It reflects what I found, not what I predicted I would find. Similarly, it is not your usual book about gay parenting. There is no parenting advice—how to deal with the PTA or how to handle family censure. In the pages that follow, I offer an intimate look at the lives of gay men who became fathers during a time when uncloseted gay men who had chosen to parent were seen as an oddity and aberration. Using their own words and stories, I examine the factors that have contributed to changes in their lives and roles as gay dads and offer my thoughts about why these changes should have a significant effect on the child welfare system and on professionals who work in the human services fields.

Usually, explorations of gay parenting focus on the differences between gay and straight parents. *Gay Men Choosing Parenthood* approaches this topic through a decidedly gay-affirming lens, meaning that I do not take heterosexuality as the norm and then compare gay parenting to that model and discuss how it measures up. In most cases heterosexually oriented men become fathers for different reasons and in different ways than do gay men. Comparisons of gay fathers to heterosexual fathers are therefore inappropriate.

No single model can adequately describe gay men who have chosen to become parents. Gay fathers, as Barret and Robinson

(2000:9) note, fit no mold, and people who interact with them need to suspend a tendency to view them as a class. The gay fathers interviewed for this study may share many commonalities, but as this research shows, the ways that they parent their children and live their lives are unique to each individual. The one fundamental experience that they do share, however, is of violating two of society's unspoken rules: that gay men should not be trusted around children, and that women, not men, are the preferred primary nurturers of children. These are long-standing and powerful social messages that, in some way or another, have affected every gay man who becomes a parent. I have come up against these rules in my own professional experiences, including more than twenty-seven years of clinical, administrative, and research work with children, youth, and families in a variety of child welfare settings. In the pages that follow, I focus on how gay fathers from different backgrounds and circumstances adapted to their lives as nonconformists/rule breakers, and how they perceived and constructed their options and their families.

It was clear from the first interviews that gay dads followed different routes to becoming fathers and had different motivations for choosing parenthood. One of the most enduring impressions that I had of the gay dads whom I interviewed was of their deep commitment to family and parenthood, despite the challenges and frustrations of living in a society that presumes that parenthood is the sole province of heterosexuals. That is not to say that they were perfect fathers. They had their own, sometimes contradictory, responses to dilemmas, opportunities, and pressures. One of my primary investigations related to how social circumstances shaped or did not shape these men's lives, as well as whether and how they took an active role in either promoting or resisting these challenges. My analysis provides a key to understanding the more general processes by which some gay men in the 1980s chose to become fathers.

Practical considerations limited my pool of sources to two of the largest urban areas with large populations of gay men, New York and Los Angeles. With the help of Center Kids, which is the family program of the Lesbian, Gay, Bisexual and Transgender

Center in New York, and Gay and Lesbian Adolescent Social Services and Pop Luck (a group of gay dads who meet regularly) in
Los Angeles, I was able to identify gay men who became fathers
as openly gay men during the 1980s. I chose to interview fathers
from that era because I wanted a long view of what raising children as a gay man has been like. I chose as well to exclude three
subgroups of gay fathers: those whose children came from a heterosexual union subsequently ended by divorce; gay men who became parents by fathering a biological child with a surrogate
mother; and those who conceived and raised children jointly with
a woman or women with whom they were not sexually involved.
The reason for these exclusions is that I believe that their experiences of fatherhood are qualitatively different from those of gay fathers who do not have a female coparent (see Bigner and Bozett
1989; Bigner and Jacobsen, 1989a, 1989b; Bozett 1987, 1989;
Dunne 1991; Green and Bozett 1991). This working definition of
the sample yielded twenty respondents.

In terms of education and social class, the gay men included in
the study are predominately urban, with graduate-level education
and in the middle to upper strata of the social classes represented
in contemporary U.S. society. Although not proportionally representative, African Americans and Latinos, as well as diverse religious affiliations, are represented in the study sample. Interviews
took place at a location of each man's choosing, usually his home.
I conducted all the interviews, which typically lasted two hours,
although several extended beyond that time. I used an open-ended but structured interview guide and concentrated especially on
the background that informed their decision-making process
when they chose to pursue fatherhood. I also focused on ways that
parenthood changed their relationship to the larger gay community, to work, to their families of origin, and to their neighborhood communities. I probed for transitions but otherwise tried to
stay out of the flow of their narratives. Because my informants had
to rely on their memories of some events that had occurred at least
a decade before, I was able to see how they made sense of their experiences and how they used these meanings to cope with the
present and make decisions about the future. The quoted materi-

als are taken from verbatim transcripts of the interviews. Occasionally, I condensed a quote or corrected a grammatical error or confusing phrase for clarity. All the men's names, the names of their children, and the locations of their residences have been changed to protect their privacy.

Qualitative inquiry offers some unique advantages over quantitative large-scale surveys. Using data derived from the interviews allowed me to develop a rich picture of these men's lives as fathers as they developed over time. They identified the themes that they thought were of most importance, so I was able to be their scribe and their ear and avoid superimposing my own assumptions or stories about their experiences. I highly recommend this methodology for investigating and understanding little known, or poorly understood, social arrangements and practices, as well as minority voices.

Little has been written about this groundbreaking group of gay men, who chose to become fathers at a time when most gay men were struggling to survive the AIDS pandemic. Although gay men seeking to become parents is a topic about which many people have opinions, few have thoroughly studied this population (McPherson 1993; Sbordone 1993). This book represents one of the first attempts to comprehensively examine and investigate the meaning and experiences of gay men who in the 1980s chose to become fathers outside the context of heterosexuality. It also is an early contribution to what I hope will become a wider inquiry in the next few decades. Another reason that I wrote this book is that I think gay men, particularly those who are fathers, have a perspective that permits them—in fact, compels them—to consider the dominant norms of a largely heterocentric society from a distinct vantage point. These twenty gay dads are important informants not only about their own lives but also about the general socialization and evolving changes evident in parenthood in North American culture in the twenty-first century. Because these men have experienced a redefinition of fatherhood in a unique way, they have insights that benefit all of us. The stories of their lives offer a particularly rich source of information about their families, about their status as gay men, and about the struggle toward adapting to a variety of environments by seeking to be a good parent in a world. What emerges from the weaving of themes and constructing of stories culled from extensive tape-recorded interviews in two cities on two oceans is a narrative of independent, determined, and nurturing men who became fathers despite society's message that they could not have this experience. Only by immersing oneself in this fashion can one begin to understand the discrepancies between the myths and misinformation about "gay men as parents" and the realities of their experiences. That we are beginning to ask questions about the meaning of the experiences of gay men who have chosen to become fathers and the legitimacy of gay men as fathers suggests that a major social upheaval is underway. Gay men's roles in parenting children profoundly affect not only their lives but the lives of the children they are rearing, as well as the lives of gay men who continue to have a desire to parent but think that they cannot solely because they are gay, not to mention the larger heterosexual society. By linking the experiences of gay men who have chosen to become fathers to the wider social and institutional context, I offer an explanation of this poorly understood aspect of change.

Gay Men
Choosing
Parenthood

Introduction

Gay and Lesbian Parenting—an Overview

Adoption, Foster Care, and Relative Placement

Many people, including some child welfare professionals, are more than a little uncomfortable discussing gay men who are the primary parents raising children. The term *gay dads* sets off two alarms. The first is related to sexism, that is, the enduring belief in our society that parenting is the natural and sole domain of women. Even modern twenty-first century America generally views fathers as secondary parents (if present at all). The second alarm is related to entrenched heterosexism. The concepts of heterosexuality and parenthood are so inextricably intertwined in our culture that the suggestion of gay fatherhood appears alien, unnatural, even impossible. As a child welfare professional, part of me loves this double challenge to our conventional thinking about parenthood. As I will describe later, some men who are gay are the primary parents of children. Their very existence challenges our old assumptions about nurturing, about gender, and about families. Using the relevant research literature on gay men as parents, I provide here an overview of the issues salient to gay men who choose to become parents through foster parenting, adoption, and caring for a relative's child, which is known as "relative care," or "kinship care parenting."

Gay fathers are a diverse group, varying not only in race, social class, age, ethnicity, ability, religion, and demographic factors but also in how they became fathers. The largest group of gay fathers once were in a heterosexual union, had children with their wives, and then divorced (Bozett 1987; Green and Bozett 1991). A smaller group fathered a biological child with a surrogate mother (Martin 1993). Another group conceived and raised children jointly with a woman or women with whom they were not sexually involved (Martin 1993). And yet another group became fathers through foster parenting, adoption, and the development of kinship ties. Members of this last group are least likely to have a female coparent, so they are the focus of this book.

How many gay dads are there in the United States? A number of authors have made estimates (Bozett 1987; Miller 1979). Patterson and Chan (1997) suggest that one way is to extrapolate from what is known of the base rates of the population. The most agreed-upon (but still contested) estimate of how many gay men exist in the United States comes from the classic work of Kinsey, Pomeroy, and Martin (1948), which found that approximately 10 percent of the male population has a predominately gay sexual orientation. Results of large-scale survey studies (Bell and Weinberg 1978; Bryant and Demian 1994; Saghir and Robins 1973) have found that about 10 percent of gay-identified men are parents. That would mean that the United States has one to two million gay fathers. If each of these fathers has an average two children (which is true in this study), one might estimate that the United States is home to two to four million children of gay fathers.

Like any such estimates, these are only as good as the figures on which they are based, and there are many reasons to question the figures But for the purposes of this study and for understanding the complexity of the experiences of some gay men who have chosen to be parents, I offer these numbers as a marker and a guide for the reader. In fact, the numbers of some kinds of gay fathers might be on the rise, even while the numbers of other types are falling. In view of mainstream society's increasing openness to a wide spectrum of sexual orientations and configurations of "family," fewer gay men seem to feel the need to marry women in order to have children (Martin 1993). In one study of gay male couples (Bryant and Demian 1994), one-third of respondents younger than thirty-five were either planning to have children or considering the idea of doing so. Another study (Sbordone 1993) found that a majority of gay men who were not fathers would like to raise a child and that those who said they wanted children generally were younger than those who did not. The research shows that since the early 1980s, the number of gay men forming their own families through adoption, foster parenting, and kinship relationships has risen dramatically (Patterson 1995).

Gay Men Choosing to Become Parents

We have been living through a social revolution, but it has crept up on us quietly. Think about how incredible, how *revolutionary*, it is for an openly gay man to undertake parenthood with an established self-identified gay identity (Benkov 1994; Martin 1993). We can assume that, throughout human history, gays have been fathers, most probably invisibly, in the context of their opposite-sex marriages. A sizable body of research describes fatherhood in a heterosexual context (i.e., Cummings and O'Reilly 1997; Koestner, Franz, and Weinberger 1990; Lamb, Pleck, and Levine 1985; Moseley and Thomson 1995; Radian 1994; Russell 1983). But none of these studies even once acknowledges the possibility that a father might be a closeted gay man. Nor do they examine the experiences of self-identified, openly gay fathers. In fact, most of the research is based in the traditionally defined, gender-bound roles of the female nurturing mother and the male breadwinning father. As such, it holds little relevance for those interested in examining and exploring the complexity of experiences for gay men who have chosen to become fathers outside the boundaries of heterosexual unions.

As I write this, three studies have been published about self-identified gay men who became fathers (Frommer 1996; McPherson 1993; Sbordone 1993). The data suggest that gay fathers are likely to have higher self-esteem than gay men who are not parents; that gay coparents are more likely than their heterosexual counterparts to share household responsibilities, including tasks involving child care; and that gay coparents appear to be more satisfied with their arrangement than heterosexual couples are with theirs. Given the sparseness of this research, however, we cannot and should not make broad generalizations about gay fathers. Much remains to be learned about the determinants of gay fatherhood, about its effect on the gay fathers themselves, and about their place in contemporary society.

Like other dads, gay fathers do not decide overnight to become parents and then go out and find a child. All parents must go through stages of transition to parenthood. Again, the invisibility of gay dads is evident in the literature. A number of researchers have explored in depth heterosexual couples' transition to parenthood (e.g., Cowan et al. 1985; Cowan, Cowan, and Kerig 1993; Cowan and Cowan 1988, 1990, 1992; Dienhart 1998), but no research to date has addressed the transition to parenthood among gay men. However, reviewing the literature on heterosexual parenting is useful, because gay fathers also face many issues that arise for heterosexual couples and singles rearing children (i.e., worries about how children will affect a couple's relationship; economic concerns; day-care issues). But gay men also contend with an array of issues and concerns that arise from heterocentrism (Martin 1993; Mallon 1998a, 1999).[1]

From the start, the hard question for prospective gay dads is how to pursue parenthood. Should they adopt? Become foster dads? What are the legal obstacles? What are the possibilities? They need accurate and up-to-date information about their op-

---

1. Heterocentrism is understood to be a result of heterosexual privilege and is analogous to racism, sexism, and other ideologies of oppression (Pharr 1988). The primary assumption of heterocentrism is that the world is and should be heterosexual; I believe that heterocentrism most accurately describes the systemic discrimination against gay men and lesbians in a major social institution—in this case the child welfare system. One of the more remarkable results of heterocentrism is that it leads gay and lesbian individuals to constantly search for a good fit between their individual nature, which Western society—including their families—has stigmatized, and their environment, which is generally hostile to and devoid of the nutrients necessary for healthy growth.

tions. It is clear from the interviews that I conducted that the pioneering gay dads had to be tenacious and figure it out as they went along, because no blueprint existed for openly gay men who wanted to become dads. Today, gay fathers have many resources available to them, including web sites and support groups specifically for gay men.

What gay prospective fathers need most from helping professionals is support in figuring out how parenting will change their lives and what they need to do emotionally to prepare for the lifelong role of father as well as the more immediate roller-coaster ride of adopting a child. Patterson and Chan (1997:254) put forward several important questions for prospective gay dads: What are the factors that influence gay men's decisions to make fatherhood a part of their lives? What effect does fatherhood have on gay men who undertake it, and how do the effects compare to those experienced by heterosexual men? How effectively do special services such as support groups designed for them serve the needs of gay fathers and prospective gay fathers? What are the elements of a social climate that is supportive for gay fathers and their children? In the pages to come, these questions will serve as a framework for exploring the experiences of the gay fathers whom I interviewed for this study.

A Crisis in Adoption and Foster Care

Nearly 600,000 children are in the foster care system right now, and 126,000 of them are eligible for adoption (Children's Bureau 2003). Yet finding homes for these children is increasingly difficult. This is part of the picture of gay fatherhood, and I will draw the connection later, but first let me describe the state that we are in as a nation with regard to children who have no permanent or stable homes. Despite the emphasis on permanency planning and other child welfare reforms of the U.S. Adoption Assistance and Child Welfare Act of 1980 (PL 96–272) and the more recent Adoption and Safe Families Act (ASFA) of 1997 (PL 105–89), the number of children requiring out-of-home care continues to increase dramatically. Right now, despite ASFA, the United

States has a critical shortage of adoptive and foster parents. As a result, many children have no permanent homes, while others are forced to survive in an endless series of foster homes. According to Lutz (2002), foster families adopt approximately 64 percent of the children that they take in, if the child is freed for adoption. That is good news. At the same time recruitment and retention of foster and adoptive families lags. Historically, many of these children have been viewed as "unadoptable" because they are not healthy white infants. Many are children or adolescents of color, and many have significant health problems.

While the majority (nearly two-thirds) of the children entering out-of-home care return to their families within two years, it is estimated that one-quarter of the children in care, many of whom entered as infants, have no plans for being reunited with their birth families or adopted by relatives or other families. This population of children, many of whom have deeply rooted behavior problems as a result of child abuse or neglect and intensified by separation, loss, and unresolved grief, pose the greatest challenges to timely permanency planning for children in foster care today.

All children and youth require security, love, acceptance, connectedness, a moral/spiritual framework, and lifetime families for their healthy growth and development. They also need stable families and supportive communities, especially in the early years of life, to form the secure attachments so vital to positive self-esteem, meaningful relationships, positive school achievement, and success in the adult world of family and work (Fanshel 1982; Fanshel and Shinn 1978; Maas and Engler 1959). Sadly, child welfare systems, and the professionals who work in them, have had an uneven history of meeting young people's developmental needs for stability and continuity in their family relationships.

It seems like a natural fit: Here are all these children waiting for loving parents and loving homes, and here is a community of prospective parents, gay men who have love, stability, and nurturing to offer these children. But despite the compelling need of the children, and the willingness of the prospective parents, a number of significant legal obstacles prevent gay men from adopting children who are stuck in the foster care system. All these obstacles stem from homophobia, that is, a belief that homosexuals are less than normal, unnatural, and even dangerous to children.

Legal Responses to Gay Men as Foster, Adoptive, and Relative Care Parents

No one knows, or can even estimate, how many gay people are already foster parents. Each state decides whether to allow gay people to become foster parents (Ferrero, Freker, and Foster 2002:21). Nebraska and Arkansas ban gays from being foster parents, and Indiana, South Carolina, and Texas have considered similar statewide policies. Some children who would otherwise be in foster care are placed in the care of relatives, raised by biological or fictive relatives (those who are "like family"), but this is often an informal, nonlegal process; no legal guardianship is transferred from the biological parent to the relative who cares for the child. Nothing is known about how many gay men have become parents through such placements. In response to the growing need to find permanent parents for children in need of permanent homes, many states have moved toward safeguarding the interests of the adopted children of gay men by strengthening their legal relationships with their adoptive families (Smothers 1997a, 1997b; Szymanski 1997). For example, if two men adopt a child together as a couple in New Jersey, the state recognizes both partners as the legal parents at the adoption finalization. This removes the need for one partner in the couple to go through a costly second-parent adoption process. As a result, when the adoption is finalized, the adoptive child has two legal parents, rather than one legal parent and one who is not fully recognized as the child's parent.

States often discriminate against gay couples that want to adopt as a couple but will allow single gay men to adopt (although only Ohio has explicitly said that single gay men are eligible to adopt). Usually, if a couple wants to coparent an adopted child, one partner adopts the child first, and then the other partner asks a court to grant a second-parent or coparent adoption. According to the Gay Rights Project of the American Civil Liberties Union (1999), at least twenty-one states have granted second-parent adoptions to gay parents, ensuring that their children can enjoy the benefits of having two legal parents. Four states—California, Massachusetts, New Jersey, and Vermont—as well as Washington, D.C., explicitly permit joint adoption by gay parents; all these states, as well as New York, Illinois, and Connecticut, have established statewide recognition of second-parent adoption. Judges in at least twenty other states have awarded second-parent adoptions. A few of these states, like Alaska and Washington, have been known to approve numerous second-parent adoptions, and it is generally believed that gay people have a much better chance of adopting their partner's children in these states. Mississippi and Florida are the only states in the country that specifically bar all gay couples from adopting (although Utah's ban on adoption by unmarried couples effectively bans all gay couples). Many states have laws that discourage adoption by unmarried couples, and agencies frequently use these laws to discriminate against gay couples.

Vermont and California recently enacted legislation that establishes legal recognition of same-gender couples that greatly benefits their entire family. Both states offer many or all of the benefits and responsibilities that are available to heterosexual couples through marriage. These states are much more likely to recognize not only same-gender couples but also their families. Recognizing that gay men can be good parents, many state agencies and courts now apply a "best interest of the child" standard to decide cases where child custody or visitation are in question.

Society discriminates against gays on many levels, but nowhere is it more clear than in the refusal of the states to allow couples to marry. The benefits bestowed on couples by virtue of entering into a legal bond of marriage are economic, legal, and emotional. These benefits are meant to support not only both partners but also their children. Because gay relationships are devalued and dismissed, gay families with children suffer from the fallout of not being legally recognized or of having to take extra steps, such as second-parent adoption, to gain legal validation. Regardless of these hurdles, many gay men have successfully created families through foster parenting, adoption, and relative care options. While the men whom I interviewed describe hurdles that existed in the 1980s, when they were trying to become fathers, many of those same hurdles remain today. Some conservative states, led by "family values" ideologues, who play on fear, ignorance, and uncertainty about gay life, use harmful stereotypes to scare others into believing that gay people should not be allowed to adopt a child or be a foster parent (See "Arizona Law" 1997; Arnold 1997; Baldauf 1997; "Court Refuses" 1997; "Florida Judge" 1997; Freiberg 1999; "Georgia Ban" 1998; A. Green 1999; Kessler 1997; McFarland 1998; Tanner 1996).

Following the currents of tolerance and intolerance in the United States since the 1980s is like watching a tennis match—the head starts to spin. Right now Florida is the only state whose statutes explicitly prohibit adoption by a gay individual. Legislation introduced in 1999 in the New Hampshire legislature repealed the law barring gay men from becoming foster parents (St. Pierre 1999). As I write this, gay and lesbian parenting is under attack in South Carolina, Georgia, South Dakota, and Texas. Since 2000, Arkansas, Idaho, Indiana, Oklahoma, and Texas have considered and rejected antigay adoption bans (Ferrero, Freker, and Foster 2002:17). As acceptance of gay men in North American culture has increased, attacks from the radical right have also increased (Hartman and Laird 1998:265; Hennie 1999).

As ethical debates about the appropriateness of adoption by gay men continue, are we losing track of the point? The real issue is that children need responsible loving parents. We must keep in mind two vital points in this debate: First, sexual orientation is unrelated to whether someone is a good parent. Second, we are starting to see results of studies of gay and lesbian parenting that show that children in these families are as well adjusted, happy, and successful as their counterparts raised in families with heterosexual parents (Patterson 1996). Even the conservative talk-show host and columnist Bill O'Reilly notes that "Rosie O' Donnell eventually will win her fight to have Florida legalize adoption by responsible homosexuals. Logic is on her side, as is human kindness, and it is just a matter of time before the legislature of the Sunshine State puts the welfare of hard-to-adopt kids ahead of fear of gays. Most clear-thinking Americans realize that it is better for a child to live in a nurturing home run by gays than to be on the merry-go-round of foster care" (O'Reilly 2002).

It is time that child welfare providers recognize and embrace the fact that many gay men and women would be wonderful parents to children who are in desperate need of permanent homes.

Debunking the Myths

Despite the recent flood of literature about lesbian parenting (Benkov 1994; Bigner 1996; Bozett 1987; Martin 1993; Mitchell 1996; Muzio 1993, 1996; Pies 1985; Pollack 1995; Rothman 1996), the idea of a gay man as the primary nurturing figure rearing children is still remarkable to many (Roberston 1996; Savage 1999; J. Green 1999). Many child welfare professionals, often undertrained by schools of social work or agency-based in-service training programs, also hold firm to a belief system that is grounded in the ubiquitous negative myths and stereotypes about gay men (Mallon 1999). Among the arguments that I have heard are that gay men might molest a child in their home; that children placed in the home of a gay couple might be encouraged or recruited to be gay or lesbian; that a gay man might not be a suitable role model for children. The myth of gay men as child molesters (Groth 1978; Newton 1978) remains ingrained in the psyche of most people, including social work professionals—so much so that the idea that gays would be allowed to parent seems, to some, incredible. These myths derive from the larger cultural myth that men in general, and gay men in particular, are sexual predators, unable to control themselves sexually or apt to sexualize all situations. Obviously, this is as true as the myth that all women suffer from hysteria because they have wombs. Such antigay attitudes, whether verbalized, visualized, or contemplated, have a major effect on child welfare professionals' work, including their assessment of gay men as potential adoptive parents. However, studies show that the qualities that make good fathers, or good adoptive parents, are universal and not related to sexual orientation or gender. Many have clearly established the need for fathers to be involved in the lives of their children (Biller and Kimpton 1997; Blankenhorn 1995; Griswold 1993; Grossman, Pollack, and Golding, 1988; Hamer 2001; Horn and Sylvester 2002; Lamb 1986, 1987, 1997; Moseley and Thompson 1995; Popenoe 1989, 1996; van Dongen 1995). One's sexual orientation does not determine one's ability to love and care for a child (Sullivan 1995). Furthermore, the desire to parent is not exclusively the domain of those individuals who are heterosexually oriented but is a powerful desire of many men who are gay (J. Green 1999; Savage 1999; Strah, 2003; Shernoff 1996).

Many misperceptions cloud the public's view of gay men as parents. Those who oppose the idea of gay men as adoptive parents use one or more of five rationales to conclude that such an adoption is not in the child's best interest:

1. The child will be harassed or ostracized because of having gay parents.
2. The child might become gay or lesbian as a result of having a gay parental role model.
3. Living with or visiting with a gay or lesbian parent may harm the child's moral well-being. (This is a favorite of judges who draw from selected biblical references that condemn homosexuality.)
4. Gay parents molest their children (based on the myth that all gay men are sexual predators).
5. The state has an interest in banning homosexuality, as embodied, for example, in state sodomy laws (Verhovek 1997; Williams 1997).

None of these rationales is justified. Not a single one is borne out or supported by evidence (Dunlap 1996; Patterson 1996).

Although the majority of the research to date on gay parenting is based on biological parents, researchers have reached the same unequivocal conclusions about gay and lesbian parenting: The children of lesbian and gay parents grow up as successfully as the children of heterosexual parents (Elovitz 1995; Golombok, Spencer, and Rutter 1983; Patterson 1994, 1995, 1996; Tasker and Golombok 1997). Not one study has found otherwise. Likewise, not one study has found that the children of gay parents face greater social stigma. No evidence supports the belief that the children of gay parents are more likely to be abused or suggests that the children of these parents are more likely to be gay or lesbian themselves; children will, in fact, be what they are. (If a parent's sexual orientation affects a child, why aren't gay men raised by heterosexual parents not heterosexual?)

The published social science literature (Cramer 1986; Groth 1978; Groth and Birnbaum 1978; Herek 1991; Newton 1978) also corroborates that the myth of molestation of children by gay men is a toxic fallacy. Pedophilia is the attraction of an adult to children for sexual gratification. It has nothing to do with the sexual orientation of the perpetrator. The most recent study examining the role of sexual orientation and child sexual molestation (Jenny, Roesler, and Poyer 1994) looked at 269 cases of sexually abused children and found that the children were unlikely to have been molested by identifiably gay adults. Of the total number of cases studied, only two offenders were identified as gay. These findings suggest that a child's risk of being sexually molested by the heterosexual partner of a relative is more than one hundred times greater than the risk of being molested by somebody who might be identifiable as gay, bisexual, or lesbian.

Myths Versus Facts

Myth: The only acceptable home for a child is one with a mother and father who are married to each other.

Fact: Children without homes do not have the option of choosing between a married mother and father or some other type of parent(s). These children have neither mother nor father, married or unmarried. In 2002 approximately 51,000 foster children in need of adoption were adopted, including children adopted by single people as well as married couples. Unless our adoption and foster care policies deal with reality, these children may never have permanent, stable, and loving homes.

Myth: Children need a mother and a father to have proper male and female role models.

Fact: Children without homes have neither mother nor father as role models. Children find role models in many places. They may include grandparents, aunts and uncles, teachers, friends, and neighbors. In a case-by-case evaluation, trained professionals can ensure that the child to be adopted or placed in foster care is moving into an environment with adequate role models of all types. This myth, by the way, is extremely frustrating to the ranks of single mothers who are raising perfectly wonderful boys without the help of a father figure in the house.

Myth: Gays do not have stable relationships and would not know how to be good parents.

Fact: Like many other adults in this country, the majority of lesbians and gay men are in stable committed relationships. Of course, some of these relationships end, the same as do some heterosexual relationships. The adoption and foster care screening process is rigorous, including extensive home studies and interviews of prospective parents. It is designed to screen out those individuals who are not qualified to adopt or be foster parents, for whatever reason. All the evidence shows that lesbians and gay men can and do make good parents. The American Psychological Association, in a 1995 report reviewing the research, observed that "not a single study has found children of gay or lesbian parents to be disadvantaged in any significant respect relative to children of heterosexual parents" and concluded that "home environments provided by gay parents are as likely as those provided by heterosexual parents to support and enable children's psychosocial growth" (11). That is why the Child Welfare League of America, the nation's oldest children's advocacy organization, and the North American Council on Adoptable Children say that gays and lesbians seeking to adopt should be evaluated just like other adoptive applicants instead of being disqualified preemptively because of their sexual orientation.

Myth: Children raised by gay parents are more likely to grow up gay themselves.

Fact: All the available evidence demonstrates that the sexual orientation of parents has no effect on the sexual orientation of their children and that children of lesbian and gay parents are no more likely than any other child to grow up to be gay. However, some evidence shows that children of gays and lesbians are more tolerant of diversity, but this is certainly not a disadvantage. Of course, some children of lesbians and gay men will grow up to be gay, as will some children of heterosexual parents. Gay children of gay parents will have the added advantage of being raised by parents who are supportive and accepting in a world that can sometimes be hostile.

Myth: Children who are raised by gay parents will be subjected to harassment and rejected by their peers.

Fact: Children make fun of other children for all kinds of reasons: for being too short or too tall, for being too thin or too fat, for being of a different race or religion or speaking a different language. Children show remarkable resiliency, especially if they are provided with a stable and loving home environment. Children in foster care can face tremendous abuse from their peers for being in foster care. These children often internalize that abuse and often feel unwanted. Unfortunately, they do not have the emotional support of a loving, permanent family to help them through these difficult times.

Myth: Gay men are more likely to molest children.

Fact: No evidence connects homosexuality and pedophilia, as I discussed earlier.

All the legitimate scientific evidence supports this assertion. In addition to the research I mentioned earlier, of the cases studied involving molestation of a boy by a man, 74 percent

of the molesters were or had been in a heterosexual relationship with the boy's mother or another female relative of the
child (Jenny, Roesler, and Poyer 1994).

Myth: Children raised by gay men will be brought up in an
"immoral" environment.

Fact: Americans have all kinds of disagreements about what is
moral and what is immoral. Some people may think that
raising children without religion is immoral, yet atheists are
allowed to adopt and be foster parents. Some people think
that drinking and gambling are immoral, but these pas-
times do not disqualify someone from being evaluated as an
adoptive or foster parent. If we eliminated all the people
who might be considered "immoral," we would have almost
no parents left to adopt and provide foster care. That cannot
be the right solution. What we can probably all agree on is
that it is immoral to leave children without homes when
qualified parents are waiting to raise them.

Support for Adoption and Foster Parenting by Gay Men

The placement of children for adoption and family foster care has,
as its main objective, the best interests of the child. Thus the needs
of each child should be the primary determinant used in placing a
child in a family's home. Issues of the adoptive parent's sexual orientation may be important to consider in this decision-making
process, but sexual orientation itself is not listed as an exclusionary
criterion in the Adoption Standards of the Child Welfare League
of America (CWLA 1988:50) or in the CWLA Standards of Excellence for Family Foster Care Services (CWLA 1995b:5–8). Section
5.8 of the Adoption Standards states that "sexual preferences
should not be the sole criteria [*sic*] on which the suitability of
adoptive parents is based. Consideration should be given to other
personality and maturity factors and the ability of the applicant to
meet the specific needs of the individual child" (116).

In March 1998 the North American Council on Adoptable
Children adopted a policy statement on gay and lesbian foster and

adoptive parenting that reaffirmed the statement made by the CWLA: "Everyone with the potential to successfully parent a child in foster care or adoption is entitled to fair and equal consideration, regardless of sexual orientation" (6).

Becoming a Gay Dad: Making Decisions

Gay men become adoptive parents for some of the same reasons that nongay people adopt children (Mallon 1998b; Pies 1990). Some gay men pursue adoption as a single person; some seek to adopt as a same-gender couple. Although there are many common themes of adoption (Lancaster 1996; Melina 1998; Brodzinsky and Schechter 1990) that readers will see reflected in the narratives that follow, some features are unique. Men who act as primary parent to a child, especially a young child, will face multiple questions about their ability to parent, no matter what their sexual orientation is. This is based purely on our society's viewpoint that men are not competent or natural caretakers of young children.

Unlike their heterosexual counterparts, who couple, get pregnant, and give birth, gay individuals and couples who wish to parent must consider many other variables in deciding whether to become parents. First, the couple must decide how to go about it, whether by adopting (Colberg 1996, 2001), foster parenting (Ricketts 1991; Ricketts and Achtenberg 1990), surrogacy (Bernfeld 1995), or alternative insemination (formerly called "artificial" insemination). Second, the couple must decide whether to be open about their sexual orientation. Although adoption by gay men is legal, some couples, fearing that they would not be able to adopt if they disclosed their orientation, opt for the don't ask, don't tell policy. Many gay men do choose to be open about their sexual orientation, while others identify themselves as a "friend" who will help raise the child. Because in most states, only one same-gendered parent can be recognized as the legal parent, this establishes, as Hartman points out, "an asymmetrical relationship between the two parents and the child" (1996:81). This asymmetry occurs on multiple levels: from school visits to medical permission forms to eligibility for Social Security survivor benefits in the case of the death of a coparent to lack of support from family members and to requirements for support and visiting arrangements in the case of a separation.

Gay individuals who choose to adopt as single parents will also face stresses that may be more common to single parenting than to their gay identification (Feigelman and Silverman 1983; Marindin 1997; Melina 1998:292). But it is not all struggle and hardship; on the positive side, gay men who choose to create families have the advantage of redefining and reinventing their own meaning for *family* and *parenting,* precisely because they exist outside the traditional definitions of *family.* They have the unique opportunity to break out of preconceived gender roles and be a new kind of father to a child (Benkov 1994).

Trends in Adoption: Dilemmas That Agencies Face in Accepting Gay and Lesbian Prospective Parents

Numerous child welfare agencies across the country have broken through their own organizational bias against gay men and are already placing children with gay parents. But by and large, few child welfare agencies seem to be openly discussing this process. Agency heads might be concerned that such discussions will attract negative attention to their agency or somehow be divisive among staff. Gay communities across the country have a large adoption and foster parenting network, as well as a virtual community on the Internet, both of which assist gay prospective parents in identifying the names and addresses of "safe" child welfare agencies where they can be certified (see www.aclu.org/issues/gay/parent; www.aclu.org/issues/gay/child; and www.lambdalegal.org).

Moving Toward a Policy of Inclusiveness

Although the historic Adoption and Safe Families Act of 1997 (Baker 1997) does not speak directly to the issue of gay adoption, this legislation signaled the culmination of more than two decades of work to make it easier to move tens of thousands of children out of foster homes and into permanent families, including families headed by gay men. ASFA provides unprecedented financial incentives to states to increase adoption and helps child welfare providers to speed children out of foster care and into permanent families by setting meaningful time limits for child welfare decisions, by clarifying which family situations call for reasonable reunification efforts and which do not, and by making the safety of children the paramount concern in placement decisions (Mallon 2000). The evidence documenting the damage to children caused by multiple foster care placements is unambiguous (Maas and Engler 1959; Fanshel 1982; Fanshel and Shinn 1978; Festinger 1983). Minimizing foster care drift and emphasizing permanency planning for children (Maluccio, Fein, and Olmstead 1986; Pelton 1991; Pierce 1992) has been a primary focus of children and family services for nearly two decades and was reaffirmed when President Bill Clinton signed ASFA into law.

Current policies have enabled a broader range of adults to adopt, including foster parents, families of color, single individuals (both male and female), older individuals, individuals with disabilities, and families from diverse economic backgrounds. In the past, the adoption process would have certainly excluded many of these groups. Inclusion of some of these potential permanent resource families caused great controversy among some child welfare professionals at first.

The trend toward inclusiveness, and a broader understanding of who makes a suitable parent, has had a significant effect on the more than 542,000 children in foster care, some of whom have waited two or three years for permanent homes. At this moment 126,000 children are waiting to be adopted (Children's Bureau 2003), and some have been waiting for years for permanent homes. Such adjustments to the system have allowed children previously considered unadoptable, or not suitable for family foster care, to be provided with permanent homes with caring adults, some of whom are gay and lesbian.

Although some child welfare agencies are struggling to develop policies about gay and lesbian parenting, many agencies appear to believe that the "don't ask, don't tell" policy works best for them. While many agencies do not openly discriminate against gay men as foster or adoptive parents, most do not attempt to recruit from this population, either. The absence of written policies and the lack of a foster/adoptive parent recruitment campaign that includes outreach to gay men may serve the interests of the organization but clearly does not serve the interests of children in need of permanent homes.

I would not argue that all gay and lesbian people should be adoptive parents. Similarly, I would never argue that all nongay people would make suitable adoptive parents. In the pages that follow, the stories of some adoptive gay dads are evidence that many gay men are appropriate and loving fathers to their adopted children. The stories of thousands of other gay adoptive parents, who are caring parents for children who needed permanent homes, remain untold. The question is not whether gay men or lesbians will be approved as adoptive parents but how publicly they will be and whether these families will be offered the same fair process and open opportunity as nongay people who seek to adopt. Sidestepping the issue of adoption and foster parenting by gay men, or pretending that it does not exist, does not protect children. It runs counter to the Adoption and Safe Families Act and prevents some children from being part of a loving family, which all children deserve.

Child welfare agencies are responsible for ensuring a timely and appropriate adoptive family for every child who needs one. In meeting this responsibility, child welfare agencies must explore all potential resources for all children awaiting placement in a family, including gay men who wish to parent and are eager to open their hearts and lives to adopted children.

These Gay Fathers

I interviewed twenty self-identified gay men between 2000 and 2002. They were aged forty to sixty-two; all had become fathers deliberately during the 1980s, through foster parenting, relative care arrangements, and adoption. None of the dads were the biological fathers of their children. They came from diverse ethnic,

Table I Characteristics of Gay Dads Interviewed, 2000–2002

Characteristic	Number	Percentage
Race of Dad		
African American	3	15%
Latino	2	10
Caucasian	15	75
Education		
Completed high school	20	100%
Completed college	15	75
Master's degree	7	35
Doctoral degree	2	10
Religion		
Protestant	13	65%
Catholic	3	15
Jewish	3	15
Other	1	5
Residence during most of life		
Rural	0	0%
Suburban	4	20
Urban	16	80
Living arrangement when children came into home		
Single	3	15%
With a partner	17	85
Living arrangement at interview		
Single	4	20%
With same partner	11	55
With different partner	5	25

NOTE: Age range at interview: 40 yrs.–62 yrs. Average age at interview: 45.5 yrs.
Average # of years since coming out: 15 yrs.

cultural, racial, and social backgrounds. Fifteen lived in the New York City area; and five lived in the Los Angeles metropolitan area. Like many gay men, they originally thought that they were not entitled to become fathers because they were gay; something within them compelled them toward fatherhood, and their lives were transformed forever.

From a distance these fathers appeared to be a fairly homogeneous group. They were originally from working- and middle-class families. With few exceptions they were well educated and had careers that helped them maintain a comfortable standard of

Table 2 **Characteristics of Children**

Characteristic	Number	Percentage
Race		
African American	6	29%
Latino/a	13	62
Caucasian	2	9
Gender		
Male	17	81%
Female	4	19

Average age at interview	12.5 years
Age range at interview	5 yrs.—19 yrs.

living. But as I got to know these men better during the interviews and follow-up conversations, I saw that they were striking-
ly different from one another in parenting styles, in the choices
that they made to become parents, and in their backgrounds.

The men whom I interviewed for this study are nonconformists
because they live their lives as openly gay men. Their nonconformity is heightened because they have become fathers. Dan, a dad
from New York, expressed this viewpoint vigorously:

> By the fact that we are gay with children, we are already ac-
> tivists. We don't set out [on] an everyday basis to be activists,
> but every action we participate in, whether it's going to the
> mall, to church, to the doctor, or wherever . . . we are out as
> gay people. When you live openly as a gay person, especially
> a gay person with children, you are a nonconformist. A friend
> of mine recently said, "You are America's nightmare—this
> gay guy, with two kids, living in the city." It is so much of
> what this country doesn't want to see happening.

Many of the gay men whom I interviewed reported having tried
to conform but failing. Their nonconformity took many different
shapes. Table 1 outlines the composition of the final pool of twenty gay fathers. See table 2 for the demographics of their children.

What follows is a portrait of twenty gay fathers, men who grew
up believing that they were not supposed to be parents but who
pursued fatherhood anyway and achieved their dream of fatherhood against great odds and obstacles. I asked each one to describe

the root of his yearning to be a dad, but the vast majority found this difficult to articulate. Each of the twenty men lives a very open life as a gay man and at the same time insists that his gayness does not define him as much as fatherhood does. But while they did not always see their gayness as a defining feature, society somehow managed to continually remind them that they were not supposed to be fathers. Also, in becoming dads, they violated the prevailing gay cultural norm. But by pushing against the closet door one more time, they found a whole new purpose for their lives.

One

The Journey
Toward Parenting

How does one become a dad? Men who have a female partner usually do it the traditional way—through a sexual encounter that, nine months later, results in a birth. In the vast majority of opposite-sex couples the woman becomes the primary caregiver. The man may be involved as a helper to his coparent, changing a diaper or getting a bottle ready or learning how to fasten the baby seat into the backseat of the car. But when the baby gets sick, the mother is who stays home from work. When the child goes to the doctor, the mother accompanies him or her. Even after a few decades of feminism, child rearing is still the domain of women in U.S. society. Popular movies and television shows regularly depict fathers as awkward, clumsy, and uncomfortable in the role of nurturer. And while we see exceptions to this stereotype, by and large fathers focus on supporting the family financially and are available as adjunct nurturers to their young children. Mothers are the ones who make decisions about the child's diet and nutrition, clothing, social activities, and even schooling.

Families created by adoption are different in many ways from birth families (Blau 1993; Brodzinsky, Schechter, and Marantz 1993; Lancaster 1996; Melina 1998; Pavao 1998). In many cases adoption was the second-choice route to parenthood for couples who struggled for years with infertility (Turner 1999). And although pregnancy and birth often include unexpected developments, most birth parents are following a known course, one that their own parents, siblings, friends, and relatives probably also took. Adoption, on the other hand, is far less predictable, described by many as a roller-coaster experience. The anticipatory joys of impending parenthood that a pregnant woman and expectant father experience are not shared in the same way by adoptive parents, who are dealing with a legal system, paperwork, and screening processes. They must go through home studies, social workers, lawyers, judges, and state laws, and sometimes international laws, the Immigration and Naturalization Service, the FBI, travel to a foreign country, and a variety of other factors. Those are the gestational landmarks for all adoptive parents, regardless of sexual orientation, and the gay dads in this study experienced them too.

However, gay dads have a very different trajectory in many respects because of often palpable interference by their families of origin, the gay male community, the child welfare system, and society at large, all of which tell them that they are not appropriate, fit, capable, or responsible *primary* parenting material.

The gay men in this study are a unique group of male caregivers. They stand out even from other groups of gay men. The gay dads are men who, for many different reasons, have chosen to be involved, nurturing, primary caregivers, in many ways more like mothers than what U.S. society would readily identify as fathers. As one dad said:

> In many ways I am more than just a dad. I'm a man, but I am kind of like a mom too! You have to be able to play baseball, but you have to be able to be tender and to cuddle and to be gentle. That's not something that most men, even heterosexual men who are dads, are socialized to do. But we have to be both dad and sometimes mom.

Pioneers in Gay Fatherhood

All the men interviewed for this study became dads in the late 1980s, a time when many—including gay people themselves—

did not consider or believe that being a gay parent was possible. With little information about how to do it, they had to create their own support networks and figure out how to navigate the system. Lesbian pioneers from the 1970s had had children through alternative insemination or had children from previous, opposite sex, marriages, but finding reliable information about adoption, surrogacy, and foster parenting was difficult for many lesbians and gays. And only a handful in the community were brave enough to create families with known sperm-donor dads or multiple-partner parenting (parenting situations with two women and a donor dad who participates in the child's life or two dads and a surrogate mother who participates in the child's life). Small support groups started to form through word of mouth, and more formal networks were created, such as the Gay and Lesbian Parenting Coalition and Lavender Moms.

Today one of the largest and most active lesbian, gay, bisexual, and transgender (LGBT) parenting support programs is part of the LGBT Community Center in New York City. Center Kids, as it is called, had modest beginnings. One of the men whom I interviewed for this study was at the original Center Kids picnic and remembers this occasion as a determining event in his journey to becoming a parent.

> By 1988 there was Center Kids, and that was a group of about twenty-five people who met in September 1988 in Central Park at a picnic. This event was amazing. There were all of these parents with their kids in the park—they had a traditional family picnic with food, drinks, and games. But what was more interesting than the actual picnic was what it represented to us.
>
> There were some people who had children already and a number of people who were interested in becoming parents. So attending that gathering was an amazing thing, just unbelievable. For us, 1988 was the year that we said that's when we would really start pursuing having a child. It was amazing because that was the point where we were thinking about starting, and that's exactly when we found out about this group. It was really through the guy we had met, who

had already adopted a child. Kevin had heard about this Center Kids gathering, and he called us up and said, why don't you go down?

At the picnic we met a bunch of people and we were dying to talk to them and ask, 'How did you do this?' Looking back, we were half-expecting them to say, 'Oh, all you do is call person X, and they'll hook you up with lawyer Y, and they'll give you a baby.' It was a little disheartening that there didn't seem to be one clear pathway to becoming a parent because every single person had a different story. Some created families through relatives, some went through a public agency, and they seemed like they waited forever. Others reported going through private agencies. A few people had gone the foster care route and had foster kids, and then the children were taken away (not because of being gay but mostly because of issues having to do with racial matching), then they tried again—those early people that seemed to have a very, very difficult time. It became clear to us that there was a very broad spectrum about how people had gotten their kids. It was all totally confusing, and it was a bit overwhelming. No one had a clear answer of how you go about it, and everyone recalled that the journey toward becoming a parent was kind of bumpy and rocky.

A lot of them were men—I'd say more than half. Maybe because it has always been easier for lesbians to pursue parenthood because they can have their own biological kids. This group of people at this first picnic was important because you made contact with these people, and even though they didn't give you one way of doing things, they gave you a number of contacts that you can make, and most of all they gave you hope that this could really happen!

Terry Boggis, now the director of Center Kids, was one of the original organizers of the picnic and was one of the parents who approached the Lesbian, Gay, Bisexual, and Transgender Community Center in Manhattan and arranged for meeting space there. In 1989 the group, which took the name Center Kids, became a program of the center, and in 1993 the Ben and Jerry's Foundation gave a small grant to hire a part-time Center Kids administrator to handle the mail and phone calls. As more funding became available through various donors, Boggis became the full-time director of Center Kids.

In a recent interview (Markowitz 2002) Boggis reflected on the twin phenomena of gay men choosing to parent and the crisis in foster care in the late 1980s:

> What happened in the late 1980s and early 1990s was that boarder babies were being abandoned in hospitals. These were children who were born to drug-compromised, often HIV-positive mothers and left in the hospital, but could not legally be called abandoned because the mothers would come back every so often to see them. Some of the infants had HIV. The hospitals were just not set up to house newborns that were often underweight and sick and needed a lot of care. Administrators were trying to find adults to care for them, but these were the children who were almost unplaceable. Many potential foster parents had AIDS phobia or couldn't handle the level of care the babies needed. It occurred to some in the foster care and adoption field that gay men might be willing to care for these babies. This was a crack in the door. Gay men started to say, "Maybe I could become a parent if I could approach it this way, if I could open myself up to a child with major health challenges."
>
> After a time, gay men found they could adopt through more conventional processes—adopt healthy infants, toddlers, school age children and adopt them permanently This happened because of the changing culture. The adoption world became more enlightened and more open to gay men. At least in New York, gay men started to pursue permanency in creating their families, and for the most part moved away from temporary foster parenting and focused on adoption.
>
> I only know of one gay man who wanted to adopt a child and has not been successful after several years of trying, and

this is in all the years we have been running Center Kids. Maybe if you live in Fargo, it's a different story and I suspect it is—but here in New York, I never have any hesitation saying to a man who wants to be a father, "You absolutely are going to be able to do this." (The only obstacle might be something in his background [that] he's not disclosing, like a criminal record, or emotional, physical or financial issues that would be barriers for any adult, straight or gay.) But I also tell men that there will be moments of challenge—hostile social workers, or a long waiting period to adopt. (14)

The Desire to Become a Father

Although many gay men do not become fathers, and may not have the desire to, the men I interviewed felt such a compelling urge to become dads that they were willing to pursue their dream despite the lack of precedent, the lack of support, and the lack of opportunity. So rare was the idea of gay men becoming fathers by choice that one father equated it to travel to a far-off planet:

Just the thought of being gay and functioning in society was strange enough. So the thought of being gay and having a child, it was just, like, having a thought of going to Jupiter. It was just something you didn't even consider—it wasn't even a possibility. So by the mideighties many of us were reaching that middle-age point; we were a bunch of baby boomer gay people, and we were all independently arriving at the same place at the same time, and I think that's what motivated the change.

Another dad offered this analysis of his desire to parent:

There is a certain amount of freedom in not having children, and it certainly encroaches on a lot of disposable income. When this happened, it was also right in the middle of a time when gay life was being revalued anyway because of surviving the AIDS crisis. I don't think parenthood is a priority to most gay people. It's not right or wrong; I just don't think normally that most people would consider [parenting to be a] traditional [part of] gay life. Whatever that is, I'm not sure what it is, I'm not sure there's a mold.

The phenomenon of gay men choosing to parent occurred at a specific point in the development of the gay movement, when creating families began to be valued. One dad observes: "In the seventies we expressed ourselves sexually, in the eighties we were coupling up, and in the nineties we are having families."

Another dad expressed similar sentiments:

> It wasn't that we all met at once and said this is what we wanted—it was just somehow we all reached that same point at the same time and then found each other. It was before AIDS was killing us off, so there was a lot of us reaching that age and wanting to create families—some of us wanted to adopt. At that time, adoption was really almost the only option—you couldn't even think about things like coparenting or surrogacy.
>
> At that point too, there were a few books coming out about the topic, mostly dealing with lesbians, including one or two female couples that had kids. The gay male fathers' groups were composed of dads who had been married before and had kids or who were currently married and not out to their kids. Being gay men who wanted to become dads by choice and not via heterosexual marriage, we were a very different group. So there weren't really any role models for us.

The families of gay men also had strong feelings, which echoed the developmental trajectory, as Bill recalled: "When I came out, I was in my thirties, and when I told my mother that I was gay, she said, 'But you will never have children and you always liked children and worked with them.' And I said, 'But I will have children,' and she said, 'Well, how are you going to do that?' And I didn't know, but I knew that I would have children."

Some men noted that their longing to be parents stemmed from their own positive experiences with family, but the assumption that gay men would not parent was a source of grief, as Don noted:

I come from a very intact two-parent home, and family has always been the center of our lives, and my parents, being the very good parents that they were, instilled in us the value of family. Family was always very important.

When it was clear to me that I was gay, there was a sadness that I could not have children and the coming-out process for me was not [so much] about people knowing I was gay [as] it was more about losing the idea of having children.

Another interviewee reconciled the desire to become a parent with living life as an openly gay man:

I came out when I was twenty-four, but previous to that I always wanted children. I'm one of seven, all my siblings have tons of kids, and I just always had in my head that I was going to have children. I just always wanted to have children. Then, when I came out at twenty-four, I thought, you know, I guess I'm not having kids. I didn't really think twice about it. It didn't cross my mind to get married and have children. I thought I'm not doing that, I'm not living a big lie or whatever, but that's what it felt like to me when guys got married to have children and fulfill that parenting desire.

So I just got totally into my career right afterwards, and then [I got] very active in the gay community. I never heard of people having children as gays and lesbians; I never heard of that.

Another interviewee recalled his grief about not being able to become a parent and identified the life event that helped him see that he could indeed become a father:

Well, it was something that I had always wanted, actually. It was probably the only problem I had with being gay . . . that I couldn't be a parent. At least that was what I thought. But that changed when I was working in L.A. and a friend was there, and a friend from college and she was ill. She asked us if her son could stay with us until she got better. Her son was just sixteen months old. We were so excited, and he stayed with us for about nine months. When his mom got better, he went back home with her and at just about the same time that we moved to New York. His leaving left this huge, huge void. So we decided to fill that void by trying to adopt a child of our own.

For many men, meeting another gay man who chose to be a father was a transformative experience: "So when my friend Ben adopted his first child and I spent time with him and his partner, I realized that I could do it, and it opened up a whole new world to me."

For others, a similar realization occurred when they met lesbian moms:

> Well, this woman came in the store that I owned, and she asked for the most natural baby formula. Sally was her name, I still can't remember her last name right now, but all the baby formulas were junk, and the most natural, healthiest way to go is to breast-feed. When I told her that, she said, "Well, I can't do that, I just adopted." And I said, "I thought you were single?" She said yes, and I said, "Singles can adopt?" She said there's a group here in the city, NYSCAC, New York State Council on Adoptable Children. And I said, "Oh!"
>
> It was just all happening in this one conversation where these little clicks kept going off in my head. I asked: "Is there any men in this group?" And she said there's two in it and that they adopted one child already and the other guy is about to get a child. So then I said, "Are any of them gay?" And she said, "Well, I don't know for a fact, but I think they're both gay." So then she said, "You should come to a meeting." And the next month I went to NYSCAC's December meeting, which was in 1988.

Another dad also mentioned a mainstream organization for singles as a route to parenthood: "So a few months after November of that same year there was a conference, a general kind of adoption conference. This group is called APC, Adoptive Parents

Coalition or something like that, and they had a conference at Fordham University."

As with other couples, sometimes one partner wanted children more than the other:

> Definitely, Bill felt more strongly—he said that he couldn't live without being a parent, and I felt, well, it's not that likely, but if it didn't happen, I would try to make something else important and that would be my life. Certainly, my nieces and nephews would be more important, which they are to many gay people—it substitutes. But my ex felt like he could not live without them, having children.

The illness of one partner was an issue that brought up the topic of parenthood:

> Evan was into it; I mean we had talked about it. He wanted to finish graduate school before we did it, but sadly what happened was he was diagnosed with HIV. And I remember the day that we got this phone call saying that there was this baby, and he felt strongly that we should move forward with it. Jamel came to us in 1986, [and] Evan died one year after Jamel came into our family. It was really tough, it was really hard, but he wanted us to be parents, regardless.

A second man concurred:

> I think Adam had the mind that I would need somebody after he was gone, somebody to sustain me, somebody to give my life meaning again. I think that was a legacy he wanted to leave me. He knew how much I wanted a child, and I think he was contemplating how well I would do with it. But the process of obtaining the kid was horrible. I was the adoptive parent because Adam was sick, he would have obviously been a more attractive parent than me, but we couldn't pursue that because we didn't want to underline that asset. It was difficult after Adam died, but I had a lot of help along the way.

Nonetheless, even well-known gay activists were unclear about how to proceed, as one dad recalled: "In 1984, I'd say, we had met

Jane Fischer [pseudonym for a well-known lesbian rights activist]—we had heard she was a gay activist, and we were certain that she must have some kind of knowledge about something, and when we met with her, she said, 'Well, good luck—I've never heard of such a thing.' So even from someone who was big in the field of gay activism and gay rights, she had not even heard of this."

Pathways to Fatherhood

The men interviewed for this study pursued various pathways to fatherhood. Some men became fathers because of a kinship arrangement. Others chose the foster care path; yet a third group became fathers through adoption.

Kinship/Relative Care

Kinship care, also called relative care, is the full-time nurturing and protection of children by relatives, members of their tribes or clans, godparents, step parents, or any adult who has a kinship bond with the child. This definition is designed to be inclusive and respectful of cultural values and ties of affection (CWLA 2000). Kinship care offers a range of options that protect children but may or may not involve placement in the child welfare system. Kinship care allows a child to grow to adulthood in a permanent family environment, within an ecologically based situation, which means that it is most like the child's own family.

Several men in this study became fathers through kinship ties. One dad described the beginning of his journey toward fatherhood this way:

> My sister has always been emotionally fragile. Marisol was single and emotionally ill equipped to care for her child. In September of 1988, when she gave birth to Marcellino, it became clear to the family, almost immediately, that she would either need a lot of help or that someone had to step up to the plate and get involved quickly to parent her child. We saw that she had problems caring for him in the most

basic ways. We have a large Latino family, four sisters and three brothers. Each of my siblings already had their own children, except for me, the gay brother. I guess it was decided, without really discussing it, that I would be the one.

The practice of relatives or kin parenting children when their parents cannot is a time-honored tradition in most cultures. Kinship care in many cases has been an informal service that family members provide for one another, without the involvement of the child welfare system. Sometimes informal kinship care is a temporary arrangement when parents are unable to care for children for a period of time. When parents have died or become permanently incapacitated, kin have informally adopted children, making a commitment to rear them to adulthood without the legal authority provided by formal adoption. In some cases grandparents, aunts and uncles, or other kin share parenting responsibilities until a teen parent matures and is able to assume the major responsibility for child rearing.

However necessary it might be for a family member to assume responsibility for a sibling's child, the dads who did so also expressed mixed feelings about becoming a parent:

> I was scared of having a kid. In a way, I was very happy with my life as a gay man. I was single, did whatever I wanted to do, and in some ways I was reluctant to let that go. But then I got to thinking: What am I gonna do? What am I gonna do in ten or fifteen years? Am I gonna be a sixty- or seventy-year-old gay man going to yet another cocktail party or an art opening again? I mean, what is life about?
>
> I just assumed, like many gay men of my era, that I wouldn't be a father because most gay men aren't. When faced with the reality of raising my nephew, I began to have second thoughts. I decided I needed a trial run, so when my sister needed to go into the hospital, I made a conscious decision to be the one who babysat my nephew for a week. After that week was over, you couldn't have made me give up that child. Having him with me made me really want to be

a parent. I realized very quickly that there was a big difference between being an uncle and being a full-time dad.

In recent years kinship care has also become a part of the child welfare system's array of services, representing an effort to place children with their relatives rather in the foster home of a stranger. Many people refer to this type of care as "formal kinship care." Kinship care has been considered a type of family preservation or a type of foster care. In fact, according to Barbell and Freundlich (2001), the use of kinship foster care has grown dramatically since the mid-1980s and has garnered media attention because it is seen as being costly to the child welfare system and to taxpayers because the relatives are paid a foster care stipend. Formal kinship care involves the parenting of children by kin as a result of a court ruling and the intervention of the child protective services agency. The courts rule that the child must be separated from his or her parents because of abuse, neglect, dependency, abandonment, or special medical circumstances. The child is placed in the legal custody of the child welfare system, which then places the child with relatives, who provide the full-time care, protection, and nurturing that the child needs. Formal kinship care is linked to state and federal child welfare laws, and these kinship homes are approved, licensed, and supervised.

Informal kinship care is still overwhelmingly the most common type of kinship care. Informal kinship care results from a family's decision that the child will live with relatives or other kin. In this informal arrangement, which has existed in families of color for centuries, a social worker may be involved in helping the family members plan for the child, but the child welfare system does not assume responsibility for the child. Because the parents retain legal custody of their child, the state does not need to approve, license, or supervise the caretakers.

Gay men who are in a position to become dads through kinship care find that it is a rewarding and successful arrangement for them and for the children, as well as the entire family. It also suggests that being an emotionally and financially available resource for one's family is a more relevant factor than sexual orientation.

Of the dads I interviewed, two were involved in informal kinship arrangements. One told me,

> The one thing that our family did not want was to lose this child to the foster care system. We had one niece that spent a brief period of time in a foster home, and it was a terrible situation for her and for all of us. No matter what, we were gonna make sure that Danielle was cared for by one of us. I was always closest to my sister, and I had a good job and medical coverage, and she wanted me to care for her daughter after she passed. It wasn't a formal arrangement—there was no social workers, no lawyers, no judges; it didn't even matter that I was gay. In fact, being gay didn't have anything to do with my being the one to parent Danielle; she was family and that's what mattered most. I didn't even think about guardianship or adoption as options—we are already family.

The connection to family and the community of origin is a boon to the child's healthy growth, development, and well-being. The strengths and resources of kin can provide many benefits to the child, while affirming the integrity of the family and community. As one form of family preservation, it allows children to maintain their significant family attachments as well as their sense of personal and historical identity and culture. The benefit is twofold, because children have the chance to stay connected to their communities, and communities have the chance to promote community responsibility for children and families and strengthen the ability of families to give children the support that they need. The child welfare system can become even more supportive of kinship care arrangements.

Foster Care

> We started calling around, and at first most agencies were not willing to pursue discussions with openly gay people who wanted to be foster parents. They didn't say it outright, but they implied it in many subtle ways.

The majority (60 percent) of the men in this study initially set out to create a family through the frequently circuitous route of the foster care system. Children enter the child welfare systems with complex, long-term special needs. As a result, child welfare agencies have found it increasingly difficult to recruit adoptive parents who can meet the needs of these children. In his classic work on adoption Kirk (1964), who did not include gay men as adoptive parents in his discussions, notes how mutual need brings together a child and family in any adoption. In the case of hard-to-place adoptees who are matched with nontraditional parents, the needs involved are highly idiosyncratic, which often makes for a more intense bond. Similarly, Brodzinsky, Schechter, and Marantz point out that "special needs kids are often hooked up with special needs parents, who for their own part diverge from the traditional agency-approved profile. They include single men, single women, gay couples, biracial couples, people over 35, and people who already have biological children of their own" (1993:184).

The Adoption and Safe Families Act (ASFA) of 1997 mandates that children separated from families and placed in foster care either be reunited within their families or freed for adoption within specified time frames. ASFA has pushed professionals and policy makers to find more effective and better ways to recruit and retain families for children and youth in need of permanent homes. Increasingly, the child welfare system is relying on foster parents to fill the gap. Foster parents, and not newly recruited adoptive parents, have come to serve as the most consistent and viable option for permanence for children in care. The majority of children separated from their families reside with licensed foster parents in family-like community-based settings.

According to the *Children's Bureau Express,* 64 percent of children adopted from the child welfare system are adopted by their foster parents (Children's Bureau 2000), although not necessarily the families with whom they were first placed. According to the National Adoption Information Clearinghouse, these adoptive placements are very successful, with 94 percent remaining intact throughout the life of the child ("Foster Parent" 2000). Thus we are beginning to learn that the promise of permanency for children and youth in the child welfare system often lies with their foster parents. This reality has far-reaching practice and policy implications. One of the critical practice implications is the need to keep the pool of foster parents growing—as foster families take on the role of adoptive parents to children in their care, the pool of foster parents will naturally diminish.

Foster parents, who are licensed by the state in which they reside, have historically been viewed as temporary caregivers or in some cases as "babysitters" for children in the child welfare system (Barbell and Freundlich 2001). Traditionally, foster parents were not considered to be potential adoptive parents for the children for whom they were caring, even when the children had deeply bonded with them (Dougherty 2001). The dads in this study are good examples of the foster-adopt, or resource family, movement; in fact, all the dads in this study who originally became foster parents later adopted the children in their care.

Some dads were encouraged to become foster parents first and then to pursue adoption: "We had gotten licensed the day before for foster care, and literally the next day we got the call. When I asked if it looked like it was long term or short term, they said, 'Oh, it looks like it's short term,' and I thought, 'Good—this would be a good way to start off.'"

Another dad recalled his initial experience with foster care:

> I met a woman who worked for a child advocacy program, a group that went out to find foster parents. They got state funding to find and train foster parents, and I went to one of their training sessions, and as soon as the woman doing the training saw me (I was the only black person there; the rest were all white), and as soon as they finished the program, this woman—the trainer, who was black also—told me to stay after the training. She had just finished telling everybody this was a long process, telling them that you might not find the child you want and that there aren't that many children in the system, and then she said to me, "Look, we need to start this process immediately. We can find you a child." The bottom line was, there weren't that many African Americans adopt-

ing children, and the majority of the children were African American. Here is this middle-class African American man, well educated, and I basically got the red carpet treatment, but I was not out at this point, and I presented myself as a single man adopting a child.

Although foster care agencies permitted single men to become foster parents during the 1980s, most gay men interviewed for this study determined early on, or were warned by other gay men who had become parents, that they should not be open about their sexual orientation:

I was told by my mentor, "You can be out, but you won't get a child." People who knew about foster care were very clear about that. And this advocacy agency chose Temper Klein (pseudonym for a foster care agency) because they were the agency that had done the first single-parent adoption. They were supportive of single parents, and what was even more unusual back then, in what I call the dark ages, was that men as foster parents was really atypical—they were letting women begin to adopt as singles, although they preferred to have coupled women, but there weren't that many men who had done it.

This agency was supportive, so when I met my foster care worker, my caseworker, and we talked, we did a lot of interviewing and did this extensive home study. We talked three times, and then she finally came to my house, and I knew that they were interested. She said about halfway through the process, "You know, it is really unfortunate that a number of people can't adopt—including lesbian and gay people." I didn't say anything, but it was her hint to me to say, "If you're gonna say you're gay, then we can't do this." I mean, I could read the cards very quickly.

Despite the discomfort that they felt at going back into the closet, most of the men in the study did it for expediency. Most resented that they had to do so but also believed it was the price that they had to pay for the gift of becoming a parent. Using the metaphor of playing the game to capture that reality, Don, an African American man, illustrated this point poignantly: "Being African American and being one of the first African Americans in technology, and almost all my entire career, I have been the only black person in the office and in what I do, and certainly that has changed over the years. I knew how to play this game, and I could play it very well, so I just went forward."

As most foster parents know, the process of becoming a foster parent brings frustrations and challenges:

> While I was waiting for my child, I was getting really dis-
> couraged. Like a lot of prospective foster parents, you call up
> every week. But Temper Klein was a small agency, so their
> pool of children was small, and I was very clear about the
> child I wanted. I wanted a child who had not been in the fos-
> ter care system very long, so I wanted an infant to two years
> old. A child who had not been physically abused, who did
> not have physical handicaps, and my feeling was, that given
> [that] this was my first time parenting, if a kid came with a
> lot of, for lack of a better word, baggage, that it would be
> more difficult. This was a new trailblazing kind of event, and
> I didn't want to add to that, so I was trying to find a kid who
> had not been in the system a long time. At that time they
> weren't letting men adopt girls, but I actually wanted a boy.
> And the reason I chose a boy was that, being a male, I knew
> how to raise a male, but I didn't know that much about rais-
> ing a girl. And given that this was a new thing, there were
> no books about being a gay person and raising a child, I had
> to be level about raising a boy. I also wanted an African
> American child. That's why it took a while.

In the 1980s, however, foster parents began to be viewed as more integral to the planning of the future for children whom they were fostering. With the emphasis on finding permanent family arrangements for children, agencies began to ask foster parents to become more involved with the children's birth parents and more frequently sought them out as adoptive parents for the children (Dougherty 2001).

Parenting HIV-Positive Children

Because the AIDS pandemic was causing panic and alarm throughout society, gay men had another level of stigma attached to their sexual orientation. Many people assumed that a gay man was, if not already HIV positive, then about to become so because of his uncontrollable sexuality. The irony is that the association of *gay* and *HIV* created an opportunity for gay men to become parents of children who were HIV positive. As Terry Boggis noted earlier, some in the foster care and adoption industry thought that gay men might be willing to care for HIV-positive babies when traditional foster families failed to come forward. With this crack in the closet door of child welfare, gay men started to view parenting an HIV-positive child as a way to achieve fatherhood. Don and Joe were a couple desperate to become parents, and in the mid-1980s they stepped forward to parent several HIV-positive children. Their story of love and loss is poignant and heartrending:

> We both wanted so much to become dads, but like most gay men, we thought that we would never be able to do that. We loved our nieces and nephews, but being the greatest uncles in the world got old quickly, and we wanted more. We wanted a family. We saw in the news that there were more and more children being born HIV positive and that their moms were either dying or unable to care for them or had already abandoned them in the hospital. AIDS was all around us—we had lost many friends or had others who were very ill, so AIDS and HIV, horrible as it was, was not foreign to us. We heard about this agency in New York called Leake and Watts that were among the first to license foster homes for HIV positive babies, and we decided to contact them. We were cautious at first, but they sounded pretty open minded, even to gay people becoming foster parents because they were really desperate to find families to love their children. So we decide to pursue becoming foster parents, [but] we didn't really even know the difference between foster care and adoption. We went to the orientation, we did the application, we got the references, and the physicals, the financial statements, and we did the

training and completed our home study in record time. In retrospect, we were as desperate to become dads as they were to
get foster parents. It was a good match for all of us.

Preparing Gay Men to Become Foster Parents

Agencies typically have not clearly defined the roles that foster
parents are expected to play and, to the extent that foster parents
have been asked to take on new responsibilities, often have offered
little training or support (Dougherty 2001). Boggis made this
important observation about the role of foster parents to
Markowitz:

> I think it takes a very different, almost enlightened being to
> be a good foster parent. You have be willing to love them on
> a spiritual level, totally embracing them and accepting that
> you must ultimately be willing to say good-bye. In this one
> way, it's a dramatically different approach to the kind of par-
> enting most of us imagine, it's not about claiming and own-
> ing. It's not about saying, "This child is mine." But you have
> to say, "This child is a gift in my life, someone I am allowed
> to love and nurture and then, perhaps, let go." All parenting
> is about that, really, but it's a greater likelihood, a bigger
> risk—it looms larger with foster children.
>
> A foster parent may be able to adopt the child, but that
> is not the deal when you go into the relationship. You ab-
> solutely have to be willing to share in the role of parent but
> understand that you are not, in the end, their parent. Just
> because you set the meals on the table and cuddle with them
> and read them bedtime stories does not erase the fact that
> they already have a mother and/or father somewhere.
>
> I have the greatest respect for foster parents. They have to
> be really centered and mature to approach parenthood
> through that channel because they have to want the child to
> be reunited with his or her biological family. They have to
> want the parent to get to the place where he or she is able to
> take care of the child they are raising. People tend to enter

into parenting assuming there it will be a permanent relationship. But foster parents have to say, "Until your parents are able to take care of you, I will love you like my own." It requires a lot of maturity to tolerate that reality.

You also have to be willing to see your home as a revolving door, but at the same time consider permanency planning as a possible outcome. I mean, reconciliation with birth parents might not work out, and then the child might be freed for adoption. It is hard to sign on to both of these realities at the same time. Again, you have to be able to say, However this goes, I am willing to attach my fate to this child's life and do whatever is best for this child. (2002:14)

The temporary nature of foster care, the unexpected surprise of falling in love with the child you are caring for, elicited a powerful emotional response from the men interviewed. Many said that they also felt sensitive to potential and actual discrimination and bias by the child welfare professionals with whom they dealt: "I remember Bill telling me that he was crying on the way home on the highway when he had this thought that maybe they wouldn't be our children any more and maybe they would be taken from us. I told him that I had a similar thing happen to me—that I had this wave of sadness and fear [that] we might not have them for the rest of our lives. There were moments when we felt that the social worker didn't understand us, and we had this fear that her issues with gay people might cloud her judgment about us as parents. We knew that we would fight for them if we had to."

Antigay Bias in the Foster Care System

The gay foster dads in this study clearly took on very active roles in many ways in caring for their foster children. A constant theme in the interviews was that social workers assigned to their cases were biased against and lacked information about gay people:

The social worker on the case seemed somewhat prejudiced and was attempting to pull our child and reunite him with a family member. Although we know that reunification is the primary goal in foster care, this family had many, many difficulties and had never shown a great interest in Josh. This social worker wouldn't let us supervise visits between him and his family anymore. Once he [the social worker] took him for a visit and when he returned five hours later, he had not had any water and was severely dehydrated. We rushed him to the emergency room, and he was held there for five hours under observation. Then the social worker had the nerve to say that he thought we fabricated the story. At that point we sat down, wrote a very strong letter to the social work supervisor, and stated our case. The social worker was removed from the case; we never saw him again, and the social services department wrote us a letter of apology.

The men in this study had done their homework; they knew which agencies were open to gay men and which were not. They also were able to identify which specific social workers were open to gay dads: "We paid a visit to Bud's social worker, who called herself 'the gay adoption queen.' She was more than that—she was an advocate for all children. We knew that we wanted a child who was African American, and he turned out to be exactly the kind of child that most needed a home."

Professionalizing Foster Care

In response to both the dwindling supply of foster parents and the increased expectations of foster parents, a trend to professionalize foster care has emerged (Testa and Rolock 1999). Professional foster parents are hired as members of the agency's professional staff to care for children with specialized behavioral, emotional, physical health, and developmental needs (Testa and Rolock 1999).

Currently, foster parents take on a number of roles. They nurture the children they foster, support the children's healthy development, provide guidance and discipline, advocate on behalf of the children with schools, mentor birth parents, support the relationship between children and birth parents, and recruit, train, and mentor new foster parents (Child Welfare League 1995; Dougherty 2001).

The roles of nurturing, promoting child development, and providing guidance and discipline are traditional foster parent responsibilities. As agencies move toward new models of permanency and recognize the strengths that foster parents bring beyond these traditional roles, many foster parents are assuming roles of advocacy, mentoring, facilitation, and recruitment and are training of new foster parents (Dougherty 2001). In addition to serving in these new roles, a growing number of foster parents are adopting the children whom they have fostered:

> I started out just wanting to be a foster parent. I wasn't positive at first that I wanted the permanent commitment of being an adoptive parent, but as soon as Susan came into my home—I fell in love with her and couldn't ever imagine life without her. When Susan first came to our home, she wasn't freed for adoption, but within twelve months she was, and we knew that we would move toward adoption. Many of our friends who started as foster parents eventually adopted the children that were placed in their homes.

Adoption

Adoption is defined as a legal process whereby parental rights of birth parents are terminated and the adopting parent becomes the legal parent. Adoption in some form has been practiced since the beginning of society. As Blau notes, whenever dependent children have become kinless, other relatives or strangers have come forward to care for them (1993:4). Throughout history adoption has been romanticized and is permeated with sentimentality. Although necessary to achieve permanency for children, in reality adoption is an imperfect and flawed practice. Reunification with birth families continues to be the principal goal for children in foster care. Adoption, however, has become the permanency goal for a growing number of children in foster care since the 1997 enactment of the Adoption and Safe Families Act (Children's Bureau

2003). The number of children in foster care adopted each year has increased substantially (Children's Bureau 2003).

Gay men are in a unique position with respect to adoption (Melina 1998:296). Most heterosexuals consider adoption after many years of infertility workshops, disappointments, and grieving. For most, adoption is something to which they must adjust when all else has failed. By contrast, gay men often look first to adoption as the way to parenthood.

As every parent-by-adoption knows, adoption entails learning a tremendous amount of information about the process (Lancaster 1993; Melina 1998; Triseliotis, Shireman, and Hundleby 1997). Prospective adoptive parents must make many decisions about what kind of child they hope to parent and how they should pursue adoption. Given these decisions, and their financial resources, they then face many different options for finding a child. Each avenue requires different procedures and obstacles to surmount, depending on the laws of the state of the parents' residents. Gay men face different implications, both procedurally and legally, depending on where they live and the adoption route that they choose.

Where Did the Gay Adoptive Dads Start?

Like all parents pursuing adoption, the gay men in this study had to learn about the adoption process and become experts on the system. No single repository exists for all the information that one needs to know about adopting, but the men were resourceful and gathered information from books (Benkov 1994; Martin 1993); from other adoptive parents, including heterosexuals as well as other gay men and lesbians; from agency social workers; and from adoption and legal experts.

The issue of openness about one's sexual orientation was a clear theme throughout the interviews. The second common theme was whether gay people could or could not adopt legally.

> We wanted so much to become parents and often thought about and talked about adoption. We always kept hearing how many children, especially children of color, were in

need of homes, and since I am African American, I thought that it would be great for a kid who needed a dad to have someone who looked like them. But I wasn't even sure that it was legally possible for gay men to adopt.

After talking about this for a long time, we met with a friend who was an attorney at the American Civil Liberties Union, and he assured me that gay men could adopt. He did point out that there were a few states where it was not legal, but in California there was no such restriction. He also told us that only one of us could be recognized as the legal parent—that has now changed with second-parent adoption, but at that time, back in 1989, only one of us could be the recognized parent. That meant we had to first decide who would be the legal parent and who would be the unrecognized parent—that's what we joking referred to it as. But all jokes aside, in many ways that was not a great place to begin when planning to become a family, but that is what we had to do to start the process so . . . we did it.

In addition to understanding the mechanics of the adoption process, it was important also to understand how forming a family by adoption differs from creating a family biologically:

There was so much that we needed to learn about the adoption process that we always had to keep clearly in our minds that what we were moving toward was going to be a very life-changing event. Biologically, having a baby allowed you to prepare for nine months; adopting a child could take nine months, a year, or even more. But more than that, we were talking about a child's life here, not just this intellectual process of being a family. Sometimes that was scary but also very exciting.

After dealing with the personal, emotional, and practical details of adoption, the men in this study realized that they had to make some decisions about what method they wished to pursue in adopting a child. For some, these options were overwhelming, as this dad recalls:

There were so many routes to adoption. We had no idea—the more we talked to people who either had adopted or worked in this field, the more we realized that we still had to make some very important decisions about how to pursue adoption. There was the issue of public adoption at a city or state agency; there were private adoptions at a private adoption agency or via an attorney and birth mom; there were issues of domestic adoptions or international adoptions. It was truly mind-boggling, and each one had different pros and cons attached to it. There were many times when we said to each other, "Oh, my God, there are so many kids that need homes, and this process is so complicated and so bureaucratic, no wonder why people don't pursue the adoption process—it's a jumble."

More than half of all foster parents eventually adopt the children they foster; more than half the dads in this study became permanent adoptive parents for their foster children. Decisions about adoption versus foster care as options to create family were clear themes for some dads as they made decisions about how they should pursue becoming parents.

We decided that we did not want to go the foster care route, even though we were more or less encouraged to do that as the easiest route to parenthood. We both felt that it would just be too emotionally draining to bond with and then to disconnect with a child if they were returned to their family. So we decided that we really wanted to adopt. We really had no idea about how to do this. We talked with some friends who were social workers, and they walked us through the process. We also read April Martin's book.

Public Adoptions. Each of the dads in this study had different personal reasons for pursuing the type of adoption he chose. Public adoptions are completed through a state-sponsored child welfare system. For the most part, children come to the attention of the system through reports of abuse or neglect. The state's responsibility is to arrange for temporary foster care if children are separated from their birth families and to work with the families toward reunification as the ultimate permanency goal. If parents or other kin are unable to resume caring for their child, the state arranges through the legal system for the termination of parental rights, at which point the child becomes available for adoption.

One dad chose domestic adoption through a public agency for very personal reasons:

> I knew that there were many boarder baby children that needed homes. I had seen stories about them in the news and read about them in the papers. In fact, one hospital in New York advertised that they needed people to come to the hospital just to hold the babies, and I thought this would be a great way to get connected. So I volunteered. The babies were so beautiful, and the thought that they lived in that hospital alone just broke my heart. When it became clear to me that I would definitely pursue adoption, I absolutely had to do a public adoption. I wanted one of those babies that had been left at the hospital.

Another dad decided on public adoption because he was committed to adopting a child of color:

> We knew that we wanted a child who was African American, and, as it turned out, that was exactly the kind of child most people didn't want. Being an African American man, I wanted to be a role model for my child with respect to race and culture—that was very important for me. We could have gone the private route, but I felt strongly that there were thousands of kids in the public system that needed a family, and I thought we could be that family for some child.

Private Adoptions. Private agencies usually work directly with birth parents that come forward and make an adoption plan for their child. Most of these children are newborns. Most often, a birth mother will approach an agency during her pregnancy or surrender her child in the hospital after giving birth. Some agencies may recruit pregnant women with advertisements. The agency provides birth mothers with counseling about their options, covers the costs of pregnancy and delivery for mothers who pursue adoption, and assists birth parents with an array of services. The agency finds an adoptive family in the pool of adoptive candidates that the agency screens. Some birth families wish to participate in the selection process, and some do not.

Some agencies are very traditional and may control the decisions about which babies get placed in which home, giving preference to childless or infertile heterosexual couples. Other agencies are more open and permit birth and adoptive parents to have a great deal of information about each other. Many of these agencies welcome single parents and gay parents.

Private adoption can be expensive compared to public adoption. The range for a private adoption is $15,000 to $25,000; public adoption costs $3,000 to $5,000 to cover legal expenses and filing fees.

This dad and his partner were typical of those who opted for domestic adoption through a private agency:

> We thought about domestic public adoption, but we were always afraid that if we adopted a child from the same city where we lived that the mom could make contact and then come back later to claim her child. That scared us. Money was not an issue for us; we had ample financial resources so we made a decision to choose the private adoption route. We had a couple of friends who had used this private agency in the Midwest, and they seemed accepting of gay men as adoptive parents. We contacted them and got the application within a week and started the process.

International adoption. An alternative to domestic adoption is to adopt children from international destinations. Because of widespread poverty, war, and political problems, some countries are unable to provide adequate homes for their children. Some are willing to permit people from more affluent countries to adopt. The availability of these children, as well as the acceptability of unmarried adopters, varies from time to time as these countries' governments and laws may change rapidly. These laws are quite complex, and coupled with issues around language and cultural customs, navigating the waters of international adoption can be challenging. Fees are comparable, excluding travel costs, to those in domestic private adoptions.

One dad and his partner experienced many twists and turns in the domestic adoption process and ultimately decided to pursue an international adoption, as this parent explains:

> In 1989–90 we attempted to adopt a child through the public system, but the looking through those Blue Books [adoption catalogs of children who are currently freed for adoption] was just so depressing and, we felt, demeaning. We just didn't see a child there that we thought we could be good parents for, and we had to be honest—we didn't feel like we wanted a multiply handicapped child, which was what they seemed to have in the Blue Books. And then we started exploring a private adoption. We retained legal counsel, and we did advertising around the country and that sort of thing. And we got a cell phone. In those days cell phones were humongous, but we carried this huge suitcaselike cell phone around everywhere we went, and we eventually hooked up with someone who sounded like a very reasonable person who wanted to talk with us about adopting her child. But there were a lot of questions in it. We spoke with her on the phone and with her boyfriend, and they're both very comfortable giving us the child, and she was very anxious to have the child. But weird things were happening to her—she was beaten up in a parking lot somewhere, just things that—extraordinary things—and it became clear that she wasn't for real. Then she just crawled off the face of the universe.
>
> Then we started looking at international adoption. We got certified, and we found agencies that would be comfortable with us and [us] with them. We used one in the city, and we had some pretty good social workers to work with. I focused on Russia because I thought Russia would have, with the legacy of communism, taken good care of its children. I assumed there would be good health and some kind of egalitarian thing. I think that was borne out when I eventually went there; it was the antithesis of what Romania apparently was.

Independent adoption. An independent adoption does not involve an agency, public or private. The task of locating a child who is available for adoption is solely up to the individual or couple, who may choose to advertise, find a child through word of mouth, or contract with an attorney who specializes in this type of adoption. Although many gay men undoubtedly have opted to pursue fatherhood through independent adoption, none of the men in this study followed that route.

The Adoption Process

Once the individual or couple has decided how to proceed with the adoption, the next step is contacting an agency. The agency generally requires that the potential adoptive parent(s) attend an orientation meeting to learn more about the adoption process and to determine what the agency has to offer. This process is also similar to what foster parents must go through. One couple remembered it this way:

> After we located the agency, we called and they told us about an upcoming orientation seminar for prospective adoptive parents. It was three weeks away, and we hated having to wait because we were so excited about starting the process. The day that the seminar was to take place was so exciting for us. We entered the agency and immediately were struck by how grim it seemed. We had heard from other gay dads that this was a good agency, so we weren't worried about being gay, but we were really thrown by how dirty and unattractive the agency waiting area seemed. Within fifteen minutes we were escorted into a conference room and the orientation began. The social worker seemed very pleasant, and she introduced herself and then asked each of us to introduce ourselves and to tell something about who we were. We were obviously the only gay couple; there was another single woman and two husband-and-wife couples. We were the only white folks there; everyone else was Latino or African American.
>
> The orientation was informative. The social worker outlined the paperwork process, the MAPP [Model Approaches

to Positive Parenting] training process, and spoke about the home study. We had already known most of that since we had done our homework and our friends told us about the process. The one thing that seemed to put us off was that the social worker seemed to be so discouraging, not just to us but to everyone. She made it clear that there were no infants, which was fine with us because we really wanted an older school-aged child, but I think if there were people who had not done as much homework as we had, they might have been very turned off to the process, which is a shame because there were clearly so many children waiting to be adopted.

The application process, which consists of the personal references, financial disclosures, and medical reports, is fairly standard from agency to agency. Agencies are clear that prospective parents must complete all parts of the application before the process can move forward. Lost paperwork, misplaced references, doctors on vacation, and other complications make gathering these items in a timely fashion a stressful experience for many adoptive parents. One dad recalled the application process as unsettling, saying:

> The application was worse than applying for college. In some ways it felt like we were applying for a loan. In many ways it is of course much more important than that, but I guess because we had done so much homework and knew in our hearts that we would be great parents, it seemed to be such an intrusive pain. The references were lost by the agency twice. I learned to keep copies of everything. In fact, by the time we were done with adopting Josh, I had a folder that is—no exaggeration—twelve inches thick with papers!

Adoption agencies usually require prospective parents to complete the MAPP or the Pride Training—two well-known foster-care-parent–training curricula. Some may require even further training in parenting and cultural sensitivity. Some dads viewed this process as a positive experience:

> The MAPP training was actually very good. It gave us time to think about how we were going to parent. Even though

Paul and I agreed on most things, at least in theory—because once the kid actually comes into your life, all the theories go out the window—there were some things that we clearly saw differently. I think it gave us time to process our feelings about some of the ways that our own parents parented us!

Some dads viewed the training experience through a negative lens: "We did a class on CPR, criminal background check, and had a home study. They asked us how much we drank, if we used [illegal] substances, if we had any issues that might be detrimental to a child's life. They have to ask us about every aspect of our lives; all straight people have to do is fuck. Sometimes the whole training process really made me mad."

Every person who wants to adopt a child in this country must have a home study conducted by a licensed professional who comes into the home and inspects the surroundings to make sure that they are appropriate for a child. The home study also gives the professional the chance to talk to the prospective parent(s) and ask personal questions about their lives, philosophy of child rearing, and the like. Most home studies may also involve an office visit with the social worker, who is evaluating the suitability of the prospective parents to meet the needs of the child. The most stressful part of the adoption process for most people, gay and nongay, is the home study. If a public agency is handling the adoption, its staff social workers conduct the home study. If the adoption is private, the individual or couple arrange for their own home study to be done. It is nearly impossible to finalize an adoption without a positive home study. Some agencies will simply rule out a potential parent who receives a negative report. As a result, the home study provokes anxiety for the potential parent(s), especially for gay parents. Gay couples have to decide at that point, and at many other points preceding this step, whether to be open about their sexual orientation and how open they can be. Many social workers adopt a don't ask, don't tell policy. As this dad remembers,

There seemed to be a lot of winking going on between the social worker and us during the home study process. She was clear that she knew we were a couple, but as long as we didn't come right out and say it, she didn't ask outright, either. We didn't feel like we wouldn't get a child if she knew, but we weren't sure what her supervisors might say, so we were ambiguous. We were clear that we lived together, and she wrote it up as if we were roommates.

Others opted for a more discreet stance: "It was clear between us that Craig was going to be the legal dad, so I just disappeared during the home study process. It was very hard and sometimes painful, but we did what we felt that we had to do at that time."

Gay men who adopted as single parents did not have to directly address their sexual orientation. They still had to overcome any biases or concerns that social workers had about a single man as the sole parent of a young child. In some cases, social workers asked gay men how a future wife might deal with their adoptive child: "Then she just said to me, she tried to steer it to gay and lesbian people—she asked if I ever thought about getting married and I said no, unless I met the most unusual, quite unique type of woman, I didn't think that was gonna happen, but I also said that I did not think that that should preclude me from fulfilling my dreams of being a parent."

One father who adopted through a private agency recalled the home study process:

Mary Moore [a social worker] came to do the home study and that had to be done fast so she came up to my town. I loved her and hated her. I think a lot of people loved and hated her. She was the reason why I had a child . . . but she's so ambiguous about it. She was worried about being accused of doing too many gay adoptions. This was 1988—so she'd run hot and cold so easily. I called her and she said, "I'm doing two gay adoptions right now. I can't do another one right now." And I just, I didn't know her, but I just didn't take no for an answer. She said, "I'm not going to do another home study for another gay one because I think I might get in trouble." She was very worried to do too many at one time. All of a sudden it'd blow up in her face and she'd come up in the *Times,* you know, as the gay baby broker. So she was very nervous about it, but I just said forget it, I'm going to apply anyway, so I did. I think she gave that line to a lot of people because she was trying to space them.

Another dad recalled the home study process as a very speedy one:

> From the first phone call, home study was very fast. We did a standard home study; they came to the home, did all the paperwork, collectively surveyed it, the house. Within, probably, eight weeks we were certified. About a month later I left on a business trip to Russia, and I was going to be gone for several months. Figuring that it was going to take a long time, I hadn't even mentioned it to the agency. The phone call came, two weeks after I left for Russia, that they had a child.

This dad experienced a more typical response to the home study process:

> We were a nervous wreck before they came. We had bought fire extinguishers, made sure the smoke alarm was working. The apartment was sparkling clean that day. We cleaned out the workout room, which we planned to make the child's room. We were ready!
>
> The actual home study process was quite pleasant. The social worker asked us lots of questions about social lives, interests, religion, about extended family, about how we were raised by our families, about our relationships with our families, and about the changes we anticipated in our lives once the child arrived. Of course, we gave great, very well-thought-out answers, which had no attachment to the reality of actually having a child in your home and living with one every day. But at the time we didn't know that. It [the home study] wasn't as bad as we thought, and we were relieved when it was over.

With the training, the application (and all its parts), and home study process completed, matches are made between potential parents and children. But the process is still not over as there are many decisions to be made. Blue Books, visits, phone calls to social workers, to agencies, and from lawyers are all a new part of this phase of adoption. One dad remembers: "We were handed a binder with hundreds of children's photos. We felt like we were catalog shopping for a child. Some were so troubled, others were physically disabled or with severe emotional problems. It was so hard to decide, and the Blue Book process seemed like such an impersonal way of identifying a child to call your own."

As the gay men interviewed for this study moved toward fatherhood, they had to overcome the first barrier, which was their own internalized belief that gay men could not become parents. Then they struggled with society's bias against men, and gay men in particular, as nurturers and caretakers of children. Evidence of this struggle was in the dearth of information and resources about how a gay man might go about becoming a parent. Each subject showed remarkable resilience in sticking with the process, despite the scant support and opportunity, and each had to become an active agent in his quest to become a dad. The men interviewed for this book chose one of three options: kinship care; foster care, which led to adoption; and other types of adoptions.

Alert to the internal, environmental, and societal forces that have preyed on "people like them," these gay dads presented illuminating analyses of the intersection of their own developmental processes toward becoming a father and the context of the narratives of their own lives. They showed particular sensitivity to the contrast between the child welfare system's desperate need for permanent families for foster children and the apparent bias against men, particularly against gay men, that is often rampant in that system. Balancing the desire to become a parent with the reality of living their lives as openly gay men was a challenge that all were ready to negotiate.

The focus of these gay dads was not on societal acceptance of their sexual orientation but on becoming a parent. Yet many believed that the lessons they learned during their lifetimes about coming to terms with their own sexual orientation helped prepare them for their journey to fatherhood. If they had to be in the closet for a period of time to achieve their goal, they did not view that as giving up anything but as a means of achieving their goal. As one dad remarked, "My feeling at the time was I wasn't trying to make any political type of statement; my goal was to have children, and if that meant that the system was homophobic or racist or whatever, then I was gonna do whatever I had to do to play the game to get the children."

One positive aspect of the negative experience of living in a hostile environment is that a person can learn valuable lessons about self-reliance and self-awareness. The gay fathers were able to use their experiences advantageously to overcome social disapprobation and create their families. Although they did not always feel this way during the journey, many of the gay dads had faith that they would succeed. And then they woke up one morning and it happened: The child arrived, and suddenly their dream of becoming a father had become the full-time reality of parenthood.

Two

Creating Family

Everyone I talked to about being a parent said, "There is no way that I can help you to even imagine what it is like."

After making extraordinary efforts to negotiate the system and become dads, the hard part began. Actually *becoming* a family is far more complex than simply getting a child, and this was what each of the gay dads discovered from day one.

The Homecoming: The Initial Reactions

After many months and in some cases years of anticipation and preparation, the day arrived when the wished-for child finally came home. The homecoming process is an occasion mixed with great emotion for both the parent and the child. Even with the best-laid plans, it didn't happen the way the fathers fantasized that it would. Dan vividly describes that day of separation and emotional upheaval:

> My initial reaction when Josh came home was panic. I was supposed to pick him up at ten o'clock in the morning; I had only seen him twice before for one hour. The agency called me on a Friday and told me I was going to get Josh, and I didn't have anything. They told me I had to make a decision to take him by Monday.

There was a lot of craziness about the foster mom at the last minute wanting to keep him, but after everything got cleared up, I finally got Josh and it was four o'clock in the afternoon. I will never forget that first sight of him—he was in these clothes that were too small for him, he had on shoes that didn't fit him. The foster mother is crying, and she just drops him and runs out of the agency. The workers in the agency bring him to me, and he doesn't know who I am—he has only met me twice—so he is shocked. And when he realizes that she is not there, he's shocked, he's eleven months old and has only seen me for two hours. It was a terrible way to begin.

The workers at the agency got me a taxi, and I have all of this stuff with me, and it was the worst thing. He was crying in the taxi, and finally he just fell asleep because I guess he was just so emotionally distraught, and we got home and we got out of the taxi, and I had to wake him up because I had to get out, and I finally got everything out of the taxi and into the house. And he is screaming at this point, he is hysterical, he doesn't know me from Adam, so I am trying to do all kinds of things to get his attention. Finally what I do is go downstairs and get in my bedroom and turn the lights off and just put him on my chest and just hold him and finally he calms down and he falls asleep.

And that evening he doesn't eat or have any bowel movements, nothing. That was Monday—he didn't eat or have any bowel movements for two days, and he finally ate on Wednesday and had a bowel movement. So we are talking about major distraught, major disruption for him. But by Wednesday evening he was totally bonded with me, but that was very traumatic.

When he came to the house I was saying, "My God, what have I gotten myself into?" You know, this was not what I thought it was going to be to have this hysterical baby.

For another father the homecoming was complicated because he was away on a business trip:

About a month after the home study was complete and we were certified, I left on a business trip to Russia, and I was going to be gone for several months. Figuring that the identification of a child was going to take a long time, I hadn't even mentioned it to the agency. Then phone call came, two weeks after I left for Russia, that they had a child. My partner went and saw the baby, called me; we talked about it, said let's go for it. Three weeks later the baby was in the house. I still wasn't there. Of course, I would get ten or twelve pictures a day by courier of this child that I was about to be a dad for and that I hadn't seen in person, you know, but it all happened very quickly. It was two more months before I came home. No, it was six weeks. Oh, coming home and seeing him for the first time was the greatest feeling. You know it was a little difficult because there was a rhythm that was already settled in, and I was not part of it. But it was what I was expecting having a baby to be. I also had a lot of free time at that point, because I was off work, so I had several months where I could devote, I guess about two months that I could really devote, to just spending some good time together.

A third dad recalled the bittersweet homecoming of his new child. He was not the legal parent, and as protection against any last-minute homophobia, he and his partner had decided that he should not be present when his partner met their baby and the social worker for the first time:

I had to literally hide upstairs in the neighbor's apartment while Craig waited downstairs to meet Andrew and the social worker that brought him from Georgia. I was so excited about the baby coming home; I had done so much to prepare for this day, and the fact that I couldn't really be part of it hurt a lot. I had my ear to the floor trying to hear their voices, and as soon as the social worker left I ran downstairs to meet our son. It was such a special moment.

Life-Changing Decisions

The child welfare agency is charged with placing a child in the best home possible, and staffers routinely ask each prospective foster or adoptive parent to carefully consider whether she or he believes the match of a particular child would be a good one for both. Like other adoptive parents, the gay dads had to make serious decisions, based on the medical records that they received, about whether to take a child into their home. One dad recalled how painful it was for him to say no:

> I had been offered another child, a very cute child, but I said no. It was so hard because I waited for so long to be a father, and a part of me worried that I might not have another chance, but this child clearly had some physical issues. There was something wrong with his foot, and he had some learning disabilities, and it was clear when you looked at his progress. And I struggled with it, but I knew it wasn't going to be the right fit. When I met Josh it was clear.

Several dads had deliberately asked to become parents to HIV-positive children. The health care challenges for these children were extraordinary, but many fathers felt that because they wanted to do it, they would be better prepared to deal with the physical complications. The homecoming experiences of these dads were qualitatively different from those of dads who wished to parent healthy children. One couple, who fostered HIV-positive children, recalled their first child's homecoming:

> Our first baby, Jeremy, was so sick when he came to live with us. He was very underweight, was having severe breathing problems, and was jaundiced. He looked like a little shriveled, yellow old man; but as soon as we saw him, we fell in love with him. He came to live with us and really thrived. The health care issues were very labor intensive, and, to be honest, they were more than we initially bargained for, but we did it because we loved Jeremy.

In the 1980s crack use was on the rise, and many dads struggled with whether they could care for a child who was born addicted to crack cocaine. Two described their decision-making process:

> When we got the call we had been waiting for, it was a Thursday afternoon, that they had a child for us, a sixteen-

month-old biracial girl, we were thrilled beyond belief. After we calmed down, the social worker, who was really great
with us, said, "I have to be honest with you, and you guys
have to think about this and be honest with yourselves: She
was born with a positive toxicology for cocaine, and there
might be some residual issues; no one can be sure. You have
to ask yourselves if you can deal with this." We were taken
aback at the predicament that this put us in, but we took
the weekend to talk about it, to meet with our doctor to
discuss it. No one could really give us anything definitive
about whether or not she would be affected, so on Monday
we called the social worker and said we were ready to pick
up our daughter. It was the right thing to do, for us and ultimately for Tiffany too.

What Have We Done?

New parents often feel inadequate (Brazelton 1992:37). Second-
guessing and questioning one's ability are universal sentiments
for all new parents. This dad recalled his ambivalence vividly: "I
was so happy but also so scared —I think I was sick for three days
after he came. I kept thinking, 'What have we done? We have no
business being a parent to anyone, we have no idea what we are
doing.' I kept looking at this little scrawny baby and thinking,
'We will never be able to do this.' But then I got over it and got
on with being a parent."

One couple recalled the homecoming of the children that they
fostered, two brothers, as a time of trepidation and humor:

> When we got our children, Jon was two days old and Peter
> was a year and a half, and it was like these bundles of joy
> were just dropped in our laps. We had gotten licensed the
> day before for foster care, and literally the next day we got
> the call.
>
> We were thrown into it with a two-day-old baby, and in
> many ways we didn't know what to do. I just called Jason
> and said, "You need to leave work now—finish counseling

your client and come home." We spent the next few months with no sleep at all.

Preparing the home for a child seldom seemed to go smoothly for the men interviewed. Most recalled having a specific plan before the child arrived—where the child would sleep, how they would cook for their child, and how they would do things, but almost immediately they had to modify their plans to accommodate reality. One couple recalled:

> The day he came to our home was such a joy for us. The first few weeks of parenting were a blur, the house turned upside down; our workout room quickly became his playroom. We were so caught up in the whirl of diapers, formula, and baby Tylenol and everything else that we barely had time to think about how Perry had settled into his own home. I was initially worried about whether or not he would mess up the living room, but within two or three days we didn't even try anymore or care.

Some dads relied on the advice of experts: "At first we did what all the parenting books told us to do. We started nesting, but then we found that some things didn't work. For instance, we quickly found that he slept better when he slept in the bed with us. We weren't sure that was okay, but after talking with the foster mom who stayed involved in his life, we found that she did that too."

Other dads literally hired experts to help them: "I have several siblings, but my partner only had an older brother. He had no idea about changing diapers, formula, or any of that baby stuff. . . . So we hired a nurse, an R.N., to help us and to teach us about diapering, about taking a baby's temperature, giving an infant a bath—all of the things that we thought we probably needed to know."

Initial reactions to parenting may not always have prepared the new parent for his new role; child care for a new baby is one major issue:

Well, my initial intention was I had this woman I set up to watch him. My plans were that I had my own business and I would bring Wade to work a lot of times, and at least three times a week I would have a babysitter. I found this woman from our neighbor, and she babysat for me three days a week, six hours a day. It was a couple months. And I expected that kind of support at work, and I expected family support more. My mother was alive at the time; she died a year after Wade was born. She had been a really good grandmother—she babysat her grandchildren and was a very active grandparent. I didn't realize that she was so gravely ill at the time when Wade was a baby. So I expected all of this family support, and I ended up with zero family physical support.

What this dad lacked in family support, he gained from the support of other parents in his community:

I totally underestimated neighborhood support. After Wade was born, the neighborhood association that I was [on the] board of directors of, threw a shower, and I never expected that. I got these oddball gifts—it was really strange. It was just foreign to them, I think, but very sweet. And I had a neighborhood party that summer, and a neighborhood play group started out of it. Wade was six or seven months old. And for the first five years of his life, every week we would change houses for this neighborhood group of about eleven families. That was an incredible source of support. It was a place to talk with other parents about diapering, feeding, you know—what's he doing at six months, what should he be doing at six months? That kind of parenting stuff, you know—general day in and day out, every week, just speaking on the phone with people and play dates. I had no idea what a play date was before I had a child. It was such a source of support for me to go to this one and that one and have them over, and I never could've predicted that. I didn't know any neighbors previous to having children. I crossed paths with neighbors very briefly; it's not that they

were boring, but I didn't go to their homes and socialize. So
I totally didn't predict that they would be so supportive,
and that was my mistake.

Changes and Stresses

All parents have dreams and fantasies about becoming a family.
Sometimes the fantasy matches the reality, and sometimes it does-
n't. Most men interviewed acknowledged that things changed
when they added a child to their lives. Like all first-time parents,
many of the men had well-developed fantasies about what having
a child would be like. This dad had a very traditional fantasy
about having children:

> Oh, God. Before you have kids, you never even see kids. Then
> once you decide to have children of your own, you walk
> around, and you become sensitive to children. You start real-
> izing that they exist. Prior to that, I don't even think I real-
> ized it. I never knew, before I wanted to adopt, that there
> were kids living around me—you see them from time to time
> when you are a single person, but once I wanted to adopt,
> then I started noticing kids, kids with parents, kids in the
> playground. You see parents dealing with their kids and the
> like. The fantasy is that you are going to have this kid who
> looks just like you—they are going to be this perfect kid, and
> you're going to give them everything, and they are going to
> grow up to be the doctor, the lawyer, the president of the
> United States, that sort of thing. Then the reality sets in.

The reality of day-to-day parenting hit hard for many dads.
Bill summarized those feelings well:

> When Jan came into our lives, things changed. We were no
> longer these two guys with lots of disposable income to
> travel, buy things, and go out to social events. Of course, we
> were more than that, but now we were dads. Parents to a
> very small, vulnerable, needy person. I guess on some level

we always realized that our lives would change when we had a child, but I am not sure you can ever be prepared for how much it's going to change. Our house changed, our relationship changed, our relationship to our jobs, friends, and families changed. The way we shopped, spent money, exercised, and socialized also changed dramatically—everything changed. Although everything changed, we didn't feel that we had less. Having Jan in our lives meant that we were enriched in many very beautiful ways.

The experiences described by Bill are only minimally related to parenting as a gay man. Although some aspects of parenting undoubtedly are unique to being a gay man, the vast majority of the changes had to do with the reality of parenting in general. The demands of bringing a child into a family vary with the circumstances. Dads who formed families through kinship relationships were obviously in a different situation than dads who adopted complete strangers from other countries who didn't speak their language. Individuals' ability to cope with the changes inherent in parenthood also varied with personalities and expectations.

The degree of stress related to becoming a family depends on many factors. Some are predictable, and some are beyond our immediate control. The temperament of the parent is a key component in this process. Martin suggests that parents ask themselves the following questions in evaluating their temperament for parenting: How well do we adapt to change in general? How quickly do we recover from disruption? How high is our tolerance for chaos, noise, sleep deprivation, intrusion, lack of solitude? (1993:217). Most parents go into a kind of shock when a child arrives. They may have dreamed about parenthood, but they could never imagine how relentless it is, how completely it changes time, space, sleep, and every other aspect of one's former, child-free, life. Most of the gay dads, like other parents, had no idea whether they could handle it, or what their limits might be, or what their capacity to rise to the task might be:

What surprised me most about parenting was how incredibly unselfish I had become. All my thoughts were about him, making sure that he was safe and nurtured. Before becoming a parent, my check, my discretionary funds—everything—was all about me, and now I am worried about do I have enough money to do that kind of stuff? And from the first day, until Josh was about nine or ten, I never slept an entire night without waking up about three to four times a night to make sure that there were blankets on their beds and that they were safe and that they were breathing, that whole ideal that they were okay. My whole waking moments were about my child. So that is a very unusual feeling to have, and the whole thing about that, when he first came in, there was not this bond between us. I think we both felt this paternal bond that I think mothers have when they first give birth to kids. There is something in that first twenty-four hours that connects them to their child—an emotional attachment—I had read about that, and I had heard people talk about that, but you don't know what it is until you experience it. It's when it just clicks. and that's what happened—we were inseparable, I mean literally inseparable. He lived and breathed me, and I lived and breathed him.

The individual child's temperament is also a key factor in the family-making process. All infants require an enormous amount of attention and are by virtue of their development demanding, but some are cheerful and some are fussy. The dads I interviewed had both types and many in between. One father had this to say about his second child's temperament:

My first child was a joy—slept through the night, ate well, and smiled. My second child screamed for the first six months of his life. He never slept more than four or five hours, was fussy, to put it mildly. I am so happy to have had the first experience first, because if not, Peter would have definitely been an only child. I always say, the second child was a very different experience from the first. I guess that's normal, but given that my first was so sweet, I just unrealistically expected the second to be the same. Boy, was I wrong!

It doesn't take a difficult child to complicate the emotional adjustment to parenthood (Brazelton 1992). Even when the dads said that they were completely in love with their child, they acknowledged that they also experienced feelings of loss, depression, loneliness, and frustration. Having a new baby is such a transformative experience for all parents. Many fathers noted that activities that they used to do for intellectual stimulation or exercise or accomplishment also had to change. Some of these feelings might be unique to gay fathers as parents. Terry Boggis referred to some of them when we spoke:

> Yes, you know, I have seen the way gay men have been challenged in this new parenting role. It's just a female, mommy-driven culture, early childhood. And the lack of welcome for gay men in that culture has got to be painful and extra challenging and extra scary. I've seen that. I've been on those park benches and playgrounds where it's all the women, the nannies and the moms, and a man comes in, and there's this kind of distrust and bristling. He can't really be a club member kind of thing. So I've seen them struggle with loneliness almost and a greater need for community. I think once they have a baby, or they acquire a baby, they are in that mommy culture. There's that commonality of mommy-ness [which] seems to negate the importance of the sexual orientation issue. Everybody bonds around the mommy stuff, but for gay dads it's a lonelier road, I think, at least initially.

Many of the dads highlighted the cultural phenomenon of the mommy-driven nature of early childhood parenting. The lack of visible male parental role models was a glaring distinction for these dads. In addition to suffering playground isolation, many of the men were approached in public places by well-intentioned women who corrected their parenting styles:

I think for most people it's very unusual to see an infant without the mom. Seeing an infant with just a man is very uncommon. But when the baby was two weeks old, I had to go shopping—I mean, I couldn't leave him home, so I bundled him up and took him shopping in the middle of the winter because that's what I had to do. Whenever I did that, some woman, usually a well-intentioned woman, would try to help me or advise me or sometimes correct me. Sometimes it was sweet, but most of the time it was very irritating. I would think, "How dare you try to correct me about being a parent? You don't even know me! I take care of this baby twenty-four hours a day! I know what I am doing, thank you very much." I didn't always say that because it sounded too hostile, but I did think it. Usually I just smiled and said thank you. The whole experience really pointed out to me how unaccustomed we are as a society to seeing men in the role of caretakers for children.

Mark, a forty-seven-year-old father, recalled his initial interactions with the community:

A man with an infant (forget gay or not gay) is a very uncommon sight in American society. While a woman with a baby engenders almost immediate social contact—baby as social lubricant, if you will—a man with a baby, especially an infant, engenders suspicion. It's almost like, "What are you doing with that baby? Where is that baby's mother?" It is almost an immediate response to a man with an infant—it's almost as if a man is deemed incapable of caring for a baby or, at worst, that he might hurt a baby through his own inexperience and ignorance. Most women are also ipso facto assumed to be competent caregivers; men are almost assumed to be the exact opposite, solely based on their gender.

Daniel, an African American dad, corroborated this experience, saying:

When the kids were younger, women always came up to me on the streets to tell me things about my child-rearing ability. They would say things like, "His hair is not right," and in black families hair is a very big thing. Or they would challenge me about changing diapers. When I first had Josh, there were no changing tables in men's rooms, so in airports or whatever I was always changing him on a table or a chair or whatever, and women would stop and say, "Are you doing that right?" Or I would be in a play-ground, and I would be the only man there, and some woman would say, "Oh, isn't that nice that you took the day off to be with your child, and your wife can do some-thing else!" It is almost as though dads should not be there and that mothers should be there instead.

Terry Boggis agrees, telling me:

There are so many damaging messages that gay men have heard all of their lives about why they can't be parents or can't be involved with children, so it takes a little longer to come around and believe that they could be good at it. For gay men, they're going to be working through "Am I going to be good at this?" There is sort of assigned awkwardness with children that all men get: "Oh, I can't have a baby! I'm a guy, I don't know what I'm doing." And, you know, it's just that much worse for gay men. They're just told for ex tra reasons why they're not going to be good at this. I just think that's a lot to overcome.

Overcompensation

Perhaps because gay dads are constantly caught between a mom-my-driven culture and an American culture that views fathers solely in the role of breadwinner, the gay dads in this study found that they did not fit into either niche. Perhaps as a consequence, many dads readily acknowledged that they were not just involved in their child's life but were, in the words of one dad, superpar-ents: "the president of the parents' association, the head of the Scouts, and the neighborhood's day care center—and I still don't feel like I do enough."

Again, Boggis confirms this phenomenon, providing this insight when we spoke:

> Gay men often feel shy about admitting they want to be fathers. They have to get past so much negative conditioning about how men can't nurture. The culture of early childhood is a mommy-driven culture. So even after they become fathers, I see gay men, even more than lesbians, behaving as though they have to be superparents to prove themselves. They are inclined to volunteer their brains out, to be the class parent, the cookie baker, the Brownie leader, et cetera. Partly they're just genuinely thrilled and enthusiastic and really ready to be good parents, but it's also because they sometimes feel an urgency to be better than any other parent, gooder than good.

One gay dad in the study addressed this issue directly:

> As gay parents we do have to prove ourselves more. I feel very sensitive to any kind of sexual joking or something like that. I'm never allowed to be with kids, you know, I'm never would do jokes; it's just not appropriate. I feel like people will judge me in a different way, whereas, you know, you see some dads making a . . . joke about some kind of sexual innuendo or something like that. I don't usually do that when there are kids around or it's kid related. It's just an example of judging; I just think I'm judged, and maybe it's me, but I think I'm judged to a higher standard. I feel like it needs to be at a little bit higher standards as a parent, which also has its good points, because I do take it more seriously. I think other adoptive parents also feel like that. I belong to an adoptive straight . . . group that meets once a month in the neighborhood, and I think we take parenting more seriously. We had to go through a little bit more to do it, thought about it a little bit more, and you continue to think about it a little bit more—do you know what I mean? Even though it took me three weeks, six weeks, you know, whatever it

took for Wade to get home, it was still a thought-out process—it wasn't like by accident I turned over and just tripped somebody and, "Oh, guess what? We're pregnant—okay, let's go!" I think adoptive parents and gay parents tend to think more about parenting. And sometimes it's good and sometimes it's not. I think it's good because they are concerned, they're active, and they're involved—that's what they're all about. There's no mistake that three out of the eleven parents of the adoptive parents group are PTA presidents. You know what I mean—they're all involved in the school and active and stuff like that.

Another gay dad felt that the overcompensation experienced by gay dads is akin to the experiences of people of color, who frequently feel that they are being held to a higher standard than are their caucasian counterparts:

> I think most gay people are more involved in their children's lives. I think it's like being an African American as one of the first in technology and all; you always had to prove yourself. I think many of us take on leadership roles and do the volunteer stuff, the background stuff, because there is a part of us that wants to do this stuff, and then there is a part that is almost like we want people to see us doing this. It's overachievement. As a black man, every day [that] I went out of the house, my father said, "Remember: You are representing this family and our race." My brothers and I were always the best kids; we never got in trouble. It was almost like we were too perfect. It took a toll on us—we knew everybody was looking at us. We were the first black family to integrate the block. We were the first black family in town, the first black family to integrate the YMCA, and back in the 1950s that was unheard of. We were taught this stuff; we were told that you represent the race: You do something bad, you are bringing down the entire race.
>
> I think that I have some insight that some nongay parents don't have. As a double minority, there is experiences

that I have had about being black and gay, and those experiences I bring into my children's lives, and so I think that
my children will be much more sensitive to these issues and
to issues about people of color, to issues around race, sexism,
et cetera.

Single Dads

Twenty percent of the men in this study became fathers as single
men, single parents by choice. Quite simply, they were at a point
in their lives where they were ready to become parents, but they
hadn't found a life partner, so they moved ahead anyway and decided to parent alone. While acknowledging the obvious hard-
ships of single parenting, these dads were also eager to point out
the advantages of single gay parenthood. One dad, who adopted
two children as a single man, said:

> I feel guilty for saying this, but I think it's easier to be a
> single parent in many ways. I see, and I could be wrong be-
> cause I'm not in a gay coupled relationship, but by outside
> observance of gay couples, you have more of a built-in set
> of roles for parenting. With just me as a parent, there are
> no roles to play, no male-female roles to play. For many
> gay male couples who are parents, what I have I witnessed
> is a lot of fighting for/to do everything. Then you have the
> two of them constantly fighting. I've seen it in all the cou-
> ples where they are both trying to be the mom and the
> dad. Whereas, for example, I'm not saying it's right or
> wrong, but with my parents my dad made the money and
> my mom did all the parenting; that was it. It was clear.
> And my father did a very successful job in money, and my
> mother did a very successful job in parenting. But there
> was not a lot of, "Oh, honey, you take the kids today" kind
> of thing. My mother was responsible, whereas these gay
> men in coupled relationships, they have to prove himself
> or something—and I don't have to. I don't have to prove
> myself to anybody. As the only parent, I make the rules, I

make the decisions, and I don't have to negotiate with the other partner.

Of course, dating for single parents can be a challenge. One gay dad said:

In the beginning I had a lot of boyfriends and brought them home comfortably and didn't think too much of it. As my kids have gotten older, there are such a multitude of issues and concerns, and I have changed how I deal with dating. So many issues come into play, especially during the teenage years. You kind of remember the discovering [of] your own sexuality so you know what it's like. And I guess I have had to put my own needs second to what I think my child needs from his parent.

One dad, although obviously delighted with his role as parent, had this lament, which closely matches the experiences of single straight parents cited in the research (Feigelman and Silverman 1983; Marindin 1997; Melina 1998:292; Shireman and Johnson 1976, 1986): "I feel very alone sometimes, being a single parent. It's lonely sometimes; it's not sex—I just kind of wanted someone to hold me and say, 'You're doing all right.'"

Changes in the Couple's Relationship

Eighty percent of the gay dads interviewed for this study were in committed coupled relationships at the beginning of their parenting journey. A relationship between two adults is a complex process. The partners always have conflicting needs and desires, all of which require communication, negotiation, and a willingness to tolerate the flaws that are inherent in everyone. When a child comes into the picture, interpersonal dynamics can become more complex (as most of us well know from our own families of origin). Parenting a child means that the relationship between partners will change, as this dad recalled: "We were so happy to be parents, but I don't think we had any idea about how much our lives as a couple would change once Troy came into our lives. We were busier than ever. We had less time for each other; our focus became Troy, not each other. Sometimes that was really hard."

After a gay couple adopts a child, many questions come to the surface, including who will take responsibility for what areas of parenting, how to navigate legal issues, and how to handle emotional issues, including bonding and attachment. If a couple already has unacknowledged communication problems, they will come to the surface with full force when children enter the family and will contribute to already substantial parenting challenges (Lancaster 1996).

Dividing Roles and Duties

Having a child is a labor-intensive enterprise, as any parent will corroborate (Brazelton 1992). Living outside the patriarchal norms set for men and women, same-gender couples have a unique opportunity to redefine their roles and responsibilities in the family according to their strengths and skills, rather than their gender. Since gay men do not have to divide the labor of parenthood according to prescribed gender roles, they have a lot more room for conversation and, as always, negotiation. One positive outcome of deciding who does what, as the gay dads in this study pointed out, is that they are free to decide what works best for them and their child. One dad recalled: "Paul and I made a lot of plans about parenting Lisa. Some of those ideas worked great, some didn't. Even though we had the usual parenting problems and stresses, the one thing we didn't have to contend with was all of this gender-bound stuff—what the mom does, what the dad does. Since we were both dads, we decided what we would do and what worked best for Lisa."

Despite their planning and discussions, one parent may end up doing the bulk of the nurturing, either because that is how they planned it or because one partner is clearly more suited for that role than the other. However, this may cause the parent who is less involved to feel left out. The child may also become much more intensely bonded during the first few years to the parent who is the primary caretaker. As Martin (1993:221) so aptly points out, the unabashed love affair between child and primary parent may further contribute to the other parent's feeling shut out. The recollections of this dad clearly illustrate Martin's point:

> After the initial shock of parenting wore off, we had this plan. I would work three days a week, stay home with Andrew on one day and work the other day. Craig would work four days and stay home with Andrew the day I worked. But even though that was the plan, it almost never worked. Craig frequently worked on the day he wasn't supposed to; because of that our bond [mine and Andrew's] grew stronger. I was resentful that Craig didn't hold up his part of the parenting agreement, but in reality I was more the primary parent. My relationship with Andrew became closer, and my relationship with Craig became more distant. He felt left out, and in some ways he was.

Nonlegal Parents

Because gay men who choose to become parents together cannot be legally recognized as parents in most states, one parent in the couple is likely to receive less validation and support from the outside world. Society may not see the father in a heterosexual couple as the primary caregiver, yet it will clearly recognize him as a real parent. When only one father is legally recognized as the parent, the other father often has to go out of his way to assert his true parenthood, which is often stressful to both partners. Both men may be profoundly disturbed because one man is left out. And the one left out may feel increasingly insecure about his role in the family if his partner is not sensitive to his situation. How profoundly the lack of legal support affects a parent differed from family to family among the subjects of this study.

Several themes related to legal issues emerged in the interviews. Jim noted that not being the legal parent caused him a great deal of pain, particularly when he and his partner separated:

> Paul was the legal parent. When we adopted, he felt so strongly about it that we decided that he should be the legally recognized parent. We both equally financed the adoption, and we had always both been very involved in the

children's lives, and the legal issue was never really an issue for us until we separated. As the legal parent, he had all the rights and I had none. It was as if I had no say whatsoever over my own child. It was terrible. I was so afraid that he wouldn't let me be a part of their lives, and he could have [done that], if he wanted to. Fortunately, we worked things out, and we share custody of our children through a mediated agreement with staff at the Lesbian and Gay Center.

Another father recalled the distress he felt when someone questioned his authenticity as a parent:

In some ways I think I have gotten used to being unrecognized, being the invisible dad. But I hate feeling that way, because, God knows, I do my share of parenting. I really hate it when someone asks, "Which one of you is the real dad?" The kids have my partner's last name, so in some ways it is already set. It also becomes a challenge when I have to sign something for the kids from school or at the doctor's office—it really gets to me.

A third dad chose to bypass the legal definition of *father* and focus on the emotional connection he has with his children: "It's hard when people question my role as dad since our kids have Bill's last name and not mine. It helps that Jean is equally bonded to both of us emotionally. Her love is more important to me than anything legal. I only get worried [about] not having legal rights to Jean in the event that something should happen, but love is stronger than paper."

A fourth dad sums up his feelings about legal issues: "People always ask, 'Who are you? Are you his dad?' Legally, we are not family, but in reality we are. We have a father-and-son relationship. Look at us and tell me that we are not."

Communication: Arguments and Negotiations

Although the need for negotiation and good communication between coparents increases once a child enters the picture, couples have less and less time to talk things over. Finding time to communicate was a challenge for most of the men interviewed, as this dad recalled:

> We were always sleep deprived and just plain tired from all of the energy that is consumed by active parenting. We could rarely find time to spend together, never mind having a real heart-to-heart talk. I had a harder time with loss of independence than my partner did. Becoming a parent was a big adjustment for me. We both continued to work, we both tried to parent equally, but one partner always seems to be doing more. We fought about a bunch of things that we never even had to think about before we had children, like whose turn was it to go get the Pampers in the middle of the night when we realized we were out of them. The first year was the hardest; it got better after that.

Another dad had a different take on finding time to communicate. Conscious of the effect that their arguments were having on their child, he and his partner became more diligent about communicating well with each other.

> There are many times when we can't discuss something right then and there. If we really get loud or start to raise our voices, the kids get this really wide-eyed upset look, so we have to wait until they go to bed or they are out of earshot before we resume our discussion. It's hard to wait when you're upset—stuffing feelings can really build up to a bigger argument. But we have recently gotten to a point where we look at one another and say, "Let's talk about this later."

Bill and Paul believe that their communication style changed dramatically after they became dads: "We used to talk about politics, work-related events, and other, more intellectual discussions, but now most of our conversations focus on parenting. I know that other people may get sick of hearing about Jason, but we, like most parents, never do! Parenting has brought us together in many ways."

Several couples remembered that their arguments seemed to focus on their different ideas of how to parent. Paul and Bill found themselves arguing about their different parenting styles and began to see that their cultural differences were intrinsic to their conflict:

> Phil is Italian and comes from a big family where food, family celebrations, and lots of what I call emotional overlap within the family is the norm. You know, everyone is always involved in everyone else's business. This was not how I grew up. Phil gets overemotional, very upset, when things go wrong, and I am much more reserved. This was always an issue in our relationship, but when we had our child, it became exacerbated. We argued all the time about how to raise our son. He believed in spanking, I was very opposed to it. I guess it is what most couples go through, but with gay men, we both wanted to be involved and we both wanted to make those decisions. I think with a mom and dad situation, it is assumed that the mom makes most of those decisions and the dads just go along with it. This was definitely not the case in our family.

One dad mentioned competition as a source of arguments in his relationship:

> Gay dads are very competitive with one another. I'm incredibly competitive, I've been accused of being too competitive, but I am incredibly competitive. I think competition in that sense can get in the way of a relationship. I see couples, more than single dads, particularly, arguing over issues of competition in parenting. With single dads there is no one else to argue with, but in couples I have seen so much competition.

Having a Second Child

Of the twenty men interviewed for this study, seventeen had more than one child in their family. Like most of their heterosexual counterparts who added a second child to the family (Dunn 1999; Weiss 1998), each of these men, without exception, acknowledged that having a second child was a huge step for his family. Most of these seventeen men waited an average of two years before having their second child. Already veteran parents, they assumed the second child would be a lot easier than the first because they knew what to expect. They soon learned the reality, that having another child can still alter one's life as much as having the first child:

> Oh, my God, having a second child almost put me over the edge. With the first child it was just me and Wade, but with the second we became this family. We were referred to as "The Smiths." I think I had forgotten, by the time Greg came, about how much work it was to parent an infant. Of course, I am thrilled to have a second child, he is so different from my first. But it was a big change for our family— we moved from being a duo into a trio overnight.

Of course, the parents are not the only ones adapting to a new little person in the family. The older child also goes through a process of adjustment. Sibling issues were another new area for gay dads to navigate: "When we first brought Luke home, Andrew was so loving and really cute with him. But once Luke started to walk around and knock down his toys and upset his world, he became much less enthralled with his brother. Like most first children, he was used to being the top child. He liked being in charge of things, and us. He frequently asked if we could send his brother back to wherever he came from."

Even the most energetic and enthusiastic gay dads had moments of utter exhaustion and wondering what they had gotten themselves into:

> My second child arrived, and he was colicky the first three months, colicky, colicky, colicky! It was a lot of stress. But it's also indicative of the difficulties of a second child after the first one. It's higher maintenance. The first one is very low maintenance. There's a lot of energy that needs to go into having two children. And there were also lots of changes—when you have one child you can still bring them

with you to places; you also have more disposable income, because there was just two of you. But with two children, life changes. Once you have two kids, you can't, you know, like go into a restaurant, you can't just hop on a plane, you can't—you know, it's just more stuff.

For one single dad a family of two somehow didn't feel complete: "When it was me and Sam, my first child, it wasn't a family unit, or it didn't feel like it to me, and as soon as they put Kramer in my arms, it just felt like we were a family—we were the Daniels family, father and two sons. And that part was really, really nice. And, you know, I said I wanted a second child, mainly . . . for my older son, selfishly, because I didn't want him to be an only child."

While having a second child brings with it challenges, it also brings joys: "Sometimes when I look at my children, I can't believe that they are really mine and that we are a family. I sometimes can't believe how far my love can go, and it gets stronger and stronger—our attachment is so deep. Having more than one child was such a gift to me. I never believed I would even ever be able to have one child, never mind two. I am so lucky."

When Coparents Separate

Gay people who become parents, like their nongay counterparts, may also split up. Problems that existed in the relationship before children sometimes surface with the demands of child rearing. Two men in this study who adopted with partners separated from their partners once the children became part of the family. Although both men acknowledged that their relationships had challenges before children, both also attributed their breakup in some part to the stresses and strains of shared parenting.

We were both so in love with the idea of being parents that we forgot to take care of and communicate with each other. Like most parents, the energy goes into being a parent and not being a partner, and we were not always good about acknowledging it. My partner felt left out of the relationship that I shared with our son. When he got home from work, I was so tired from parenting that I didn't have the strength to give him the attention that I had before children.

Feeling emotionally deprived and excluded is painful. Another person who comes along offering affection, attention, and comfort may make a partner vulnerable to an affair, or his arrival on the scene may lead to anger and resentment, which can be toxic to the relationship. Some couples seek support and assistance from the mental health community, as Joe and James did:

> We had a lot of conflicts in our relationship when we became parents. Money issues, scheduling issues, parenting styles were all issues. Our sex life had deteriorated, and our communication had broken down. We needed tools to help us reconnect. We went to a therapist, someone who understood gay people and parenting issues. It really saved our relationship and made us better parents too. It wasn't as easy as I am making it seem; it was a lot of work, but it was worth it.

When a couple relationship ended, the family relationships were reconfigured to create a responsible parenting plan:

> When we finally decided to separate after a lot of painful discussion, once again, we had to figure out everything about being divorced gay parents by ourselves. It's not like with straight couples, where they can go to an attorney and have someone mediate the separation agreement. Since gay people do not have sanctioned, legally recognized, unions, they once again have to figure out how to do things without sanctioned legal guidance. No one we knew had ever had to figure out how to develop a separation agreement with a gay couple that had children. We now had to learn to be coparents who lived separately. It's really hard to work out an amicable agreement with someone who you used to love, especially when you are really angry with them, but you have to forget your own pain and focus on being a good parent.

Terry Boggis suggests that there are differences in separation for gay men and lesbians:

> Where I see the difference is the way men separate who have kids. I think they have done a much better job at separating than the women. And I think mostly, and I'm not really sure, I've thought about this a lot over the years because I've just seen so much of it, the coming apart, that men are much more stand-up about it than women have been. I think it has to do with biology, I think in many of the lesbian households one is the biological mother and the other, the non-bio mom gets the shaft and for gay men most of them opt for adoption and so there's no entitlements based on biology, I mean most one-upmanship is around entitlement. But I also think it goes back to the same issue of men not being socialized to expect some sort of primary access to children so that when it's time to separate—you know men being sort of grateful for that access, whatever they get, so they're sort of more generous I think about the terms when they separate. For most men they feel, I'm so happy that I never expected these riches in my life. But there's something less about claiming the children like territory, like property, so I'd say there is a big difference in the separations that men with children experience. (Markowitz 2002:16)

Brodzinsky, Schechter, and Marantz (1993) found that all children, whether they had been formally adopted or not, were similarly affected by the separation and divorce of their parents. Although the breakup of a relationship is always disruptive to the couple and to the children involved, the gay men in this study who experienced separation kept the well-being of their children as their primary focus.

Career

Men in Western society are traditionally defined through their relationship to work and commitment to developing their careers (Yankelovitch 1974). In the mainstream literature on fathers (Barnett and Baruch 1988; Baruch and Barnett 1983; Hetherington and Stanley-Hagan 1997; Hochschild 1995; Hosley and Montemayor 1997; Knibiehler 1995; Lamb 1986, 1987, 1997; Lamb, Pleck, and Levine 1985; Lewis 1997; Lewis and Weintraub 1976; Pleck 1982), most are clearly defined in their role as breadwinner. Although economic security was certainly a factor for all the men I interviewed, all the dads in this study acknowledged changes in their commitment to their career as a result of becoming a parent. This dad summarized the sentiments of many:

> Oh, my God, my relationship to work changed entirely when I became a parent.
>
> The way my world at work changed was like what happens to any person who becomes a parent; your life changes dramatically. Obviously, my career did suffer. When the company knows that an employee cannot be there for really crucial things, they stop asking you to do things. I tried to stay as engaged as possible and worked odd hours to try to make up for the times when I wasn't there. But, yes, my attitude toward work changed, and my career did suffer.
>
> I initially took off two weeks when Josh came home. I wish I had taken off much more time. Financially, I just wanted to make sure I was all right. I remember at the end of those two weeks, I was so wrapped up in this life, your child, and after that point it's like you are in this fairy-tale world, and then you have to go back to work. I remember going to work that first day and thinking, "This is so bizarre in that when I had left, everything at work seemed to be such a reality to me, but now what was reality was at home." I wish I had had the luxury of staying at home and tending to my baby, but I couldn't have done that.

Juggling work and family were prominent themes for the working dads:

> My work schedule was tough, and trying to juggle my work schedule and having a family was very tough. I took

a lot of days off, and now obviously corporations have moved in a more family-positive way and have a clear understanding, but when I first became a parent, I think I was the first man who was taking family leave time. This was usually something that women staff did, not men. If I had family-friendly policies at work then, I would have been at work more often. I took many more sick days, I took more personal days, and other people were doing that too, but they were mostly women back then. I think men were not asserting their roles in taking . . . more lead-parenting roles. I think we see more of that now. Like, for example, the guy that I work with just took a paternity leave for three months after adopting a kid, and you see more of that now. But back in the eighties men didn't do that; I guess gay men were really trailblazers in that sense.

Several men had their own businesses, and while their attitudes toward work changed, the flexibility that they experienced as business owners permitted them to have more flexible parenting arrangements:

I owned my own business. I often say that my father was a workaholic. He worked six days a week, and all my brothers worked six days a week and let their wives parent. As soon as I became a parent, I only had a babysitter [for] three 6-hour days a week; for two days a week, I was with Wilson. I would bring him to work, I would stop in and answer the phone, but it really wasn't working full time. I would go in at night sometimes, put him in the crib, sleeping at night, and stocking shelves and doing things at night. So I was putting in hours when I worked; a lot of times I worked much less, and I have worked much less ever since my second child. I'm usually home when they get off the bus and [I'm] making dinner. I put them on the bus in the morning; I'm a full-time parent, and it is what I do. I feel very blessed because I don't think I'd have really much of a relationship with my kids, if I had to be straight and I had to, you know, be the breadwinner. So I feel very lucky to be gay and have a relationship with my kids.

Many dads encountered a mixed response to their parenthood, but most were positive:

> Well, first of all, I think it was interesting the response that I got at work—there were people who quietly did not approve of me adopting a child, and then there were these other people who were actually very supportive. My office threw me a shower after we got Josh. My manager wrote me this *incredible, raving* letter about me to the agency, you know, when you have to get those letters of recommendation for the home study process. I think I even kept it.

Like other parents, gay dads found that they were less available to socialize with coworkers than before they became a parent. One dad remembered:

> Yes, I had less time to be social, and I think that's probably the biggest thing because there's a lot less time to be social. I did a lot more paperwork at home than I did. . . . Otherwise, I might stay in the office until midnight or one in the morning, doing paperwork, whereas when I became a parent, I took it home. I took the baby to a lot of meetings rather than having to find a babysitter. But I took him to a lot of meetings in a carrier and so I got through. But I think probably the biggest thing was doing all the social things with work, and that I consolidated a lot more things once babies arrived.

One dad disagreed with the others, saying that his commitment to work did not change, but he does acknowledge his own addiction to work:

> The [work] hours were around the clock, literally, seven days a week. It was a high-stress environment—we reorganized large banks. It was a politically intense environment; people's jobs are on the line, and we were dealing with all levels, from the board of directors down to the clerks. The strain—emotional strain—with what was happening. I think Nate was a joy, but I don't think he changed the nature of work. Subsequently other considerations were what

changed things—how to arrange child care, for example.
I've always been a workaholic, and I always worked into the
night, that's just my nature.

Relationship to the Gay Community

Friendships frequently change when children enter the picture.
Commitments to friends in the gay and lesbian community are often strong and of the quality and type that some describe as fictive
kin (Riley 1988; Weston 1991). The friendships of many gay men
ran the gamut, from those who rejoiced with the new parents and
wanted to share their joy at becoming parents to those who were
aghast at the idea of including children at any social event and who
eventually dropped the friendship because of the children.

The experience of coming out as dads to friends, both gay and
nongay, and dealing with their reactions was usually a mixed one:
"I discussed it with friends, but the reaction from mostly gay men
was pretty negative, I thought. Some straight people were supportive, and they would say, 'Oh, that's great! You'd be great parents.' Some people reacted like, 'Oh, why would you want to do
that?' So it was a mix, but with gay men it was usually like—
'What are you trying to do? Be straight people?' It was totally in-
comprehensible to them."

Another dad recalls the reaction from his gay community when
he became a parent:

> My relationship with the gay community after I adopted
> was awful. Again, when you are a trailblazer like this, peo-
> ple have to get up to speed, and no one was up to speed on
> this. I remember going out to restaurants—I lived in a gay
> world, all my friends were gay, and so the restaurants I went
> to were gay, and I remember going to these restaurants with
> Josh and having people give me these disapproving looks. I
> remember once, Mark and I were going on a three- or four-
> day vacation, and we were going to Rehoboth Beach, and we
> couldn't find a gay place that would take us with a child.
> We had a confirmed reservation and then called to confirm

and just make sure that they knew we were coming with a kid, and as soon as they found out, they would say, "Oh, your reservation has been taken."

Many gay men acknowledged losing friends in the gay community once they had children:

Gay friends, um, I lost a number of gay friends which, in retrospect, I realized, but at the time I didn't realize, that I would. Everybody at first was sort of, "Oh, that's sweet, that's cool, blah, blah, blah," but when push came to shove and you had a baby, and you couldn't do the bar scene all the time—you know, a lot of them were bar men that you thought were really intimate, but then you realized were not, you know. Because you're not at the bar anymore, you're not doing anything else with them. So those all dropped by the wayside, and also many of my political friends I also lost. So they fell by the wayside just because of logistics and, you know, it's the classic straight thing too: When you have kids, your single friends, even if you're straight, your single friends sort of fall by the wayside unless they somehow can take an interest in your kids and in your new family And some did, some didn't. So some stayed but not a lot. My old friends would say, "Oh, how's Wade?" Sort of feigned an interest, but they're really not that interested.

One dad said he lost friendships because of gender issues:

The biggest surprise was that a certain amount of single female friends . . . chose to end our friendships, [they] just did not think it [adoption] was something that I should do. They chose to terminate our friendships. One extremely hard personal change was my closest friend who was a woman; she just thought it was so wrong. She couldn't deal with the change. It was very painful.

Another dad said that age was a factor: "As I said, some were very supportive, generally the younger ones; many of my older

friends were appalled. I did lose some of those over it, but it did-
n't matter to me." The supportive response from his gay friends
was what this dad recalled: "Of course, some friends who were gay
were just horrified at the thought of having children in our social
circle, [but] the majority of my friends were wonderfully supportive. They were eager to be uncles. Actually, very few of them
had experience with children, but several of them tried very hard
to be good uncles and to get involved in the children's lives."

One of the most common criticisms leveled at gay men by their
gay communities was that they had sold out to the straight world
or were trying somehow to be just like straights: "The whole gay
community is about creating family, but sometimes kids don't fit
into the gay community. Like we went to Gay Day at a local
amusement park, and all the kids' rides were closed! Then we
went to a gay dads' picnic. We swapped car seat and day care stories. Were we mimicking straight parents or was this just the story of being a parent?"

For many gay men the loss of long-time friends was painful, and
others had a strange feeling of going into exile. They had been entrenched in the gay world for so long, and now they were outsiders:

> I didn't have a lot of straight friends at that point. I was
> very, very active politically in the gay community, and I had
> pretty much surrounded myself with gay men. I had a busi-
> ness, so clearly I was around nongay people, but socially I
> pretty much socialized with one hundred percent gay peo-
> ple. I just totally immersed myself in the gay community
> and was going out six nights a week. I was just totally, to-
> tally immersed in the gay community, so straight friends? I
> didn't have that many.

Estrangement from the gay community after children, painful
as it was, led many gay dads to connect with the heterosexual
world in a way that they never imagined:

> My world was kind of shattered because I had to introduce
> myself to the straight world, and what happened was, we
> did all the things that I normally wouldn't do. We went to

Puerto Rico one year with Josh. We decided to stay in a regular traditional hotel rather than a guest house because they had many more facilities for us. The hotel is used to children; the guest houses are not used to children. That's what happened—we started to go to family restaurants. I didn't know these places. Who knew of family restaurants? We used to go to this horrible restaurant, but they had great things for kids and they loved it—I think it was called the Ground Round. We would also go to McDonald's or any place that welcomes children. I never knew those places existed—you see them as a parentless person, but you don't go into them, or if you go to McDonald's, you go get a hamburger and you're on your way. You don't go to the play park. I didn't really have any interest in going to Disney World or any of those things, but when you have kids, it opens a whole new arena. When I think about all of those things we did when they were younger, going down to Madison Square Garden to see *Sesame Street Live,* or going to see the *Ninja Turtles Live.* When we took the kids to see Radio City Music Hall's Christmas Show and when I looked over and Josh saw Santa Claus go up in the sky at the end, and his mouth dropped! It was such an unbelievable feeling. Or the first time we had a Christmas tree when he was two and much more aware of Christmas and presents and him and Mark had made cookies and he saw that Santa had eaten his cookies and drank the milk, and he saw all of these presents and he just, he was just ecstatic—those are the kinds of experiences that make it all worthwhile, all the aggravation, all the whatever the stress of parenting. It's wiped away.

In commenting about the difference between gay men with children and gay men without children, one dad drew this distinction:

I don't think those gay people who don't want children are so different from those straight people who don't want children. I think that there are some people who just don't want to make that commitment. It's a lifetime commitment, and they have worked on themselves, they have developed their careers, they have a relationship or whatever, and there is no room in their lives for children, which entails taking a part of themselves and giving it to another. This is for gay and straight and I think that's fine; I think they should do what they have to do. And then there are these people, gay and straight, who raise children and who just shouldn't do it. The difference in our situation is that we can't just create children—well, we can, but most don't—but there is more of a pressure on straight people to have children than there is for us.

Another gay dad attributed the difference between gays who do and don't want to have children to a phenomenon that is more societally driven:

I think that a significant thing is that we have been led into society; our generation had to deal with some incredible adverse situations in society [because] the society was so repressive to us, saying that we were immoral people, that we are horrible people, that we are against God, and sin and the Bible and all that. So many of us have that ingrained in us, and I think to some level, that self- hatred, that internalized homophobia, is so ingrained that we start believing that stuff about ourselves. And when you believe it, the ideal of having children, which represents the whole, the continuation of society, the creation of civilization, that that is so ingrained, that we are not supposed to be a part of that. But I find that for many people that is one reason that they don't want to have kids, or it is their own personal experience of having such a negative experience in their own personal lives with their families that keeps them from having children. For some gay people it is too difficult to be a parent.

A third dad agreed, commenting: "I don't think parenthood is a priority to most gay people. It's not right or wrong; I just don't think it's typical—it's not something that most people would consider a traditional gay lifestyle—whatever that is, I'm not sure what it is, I'm not sure there's a mold."

The sacrifices, the changes, the losses of friendship—all seemed worth it to the men I interviewed:

> The thing I observed about people who want children in their lives is that people who really enjoy being a part of the delicate child's life enjoy children. I felt that the various sacrifices are worth it just in order to be a part of the development of a child's life. I don't think the choices are all that different from what a straight person would do. I think it's making a conscious—it's part of making a conscious effort to be a dad. Just because you want get a child, you really want to be a part of who that child, to be a part of who that child becomes.

Most of the fathers whom I interviewed realized that they needed to have a social life and connect with other adults after they had children. Many found that their social worlds ceased being exclusively gay but expanded to include heterosexual singles and couples, with the collective connection to one another being children, not sexual orientation.

Family-of-Origin Reactions

It's true that not all straight people meet with family approval when they bring home a potential spouse, but usually when a child comes into the picture, family members soften their position and become united in their love for the child. Gay dads in general face less certainty that their families will support their decision to become a parent. Although the men I interviewed reported a range of experiences, the overwhelming majority reported that their families of origin were very supportive of their decision to become parents.

Of course, some families were initially shocked by their gay child's decision to become a father:

> At first my parents were taken aback. They just kept saying, "We don't get it, I thought gay people didn't want to have children?" They kept telling me how hard it was go-

ing to be and asked if I was sure. After they realized that we had done our homework and had given this parenting thing a great deal of thought, they were very supportive and have been great grandparents to Tanya. I have been very fortunate; I have a very loving family.

Some men recalled how their parents seemed to feel the need to warn them about the labor-intensive nature of parenting: "When I told my father, after we had everything in process, that we were going to adopt, he at first said, 'Are you sure this is what you want to do?' When I told him yes, he said, 'Well, then, great, but be prepared to give up a lot of things that you used to do for yourself. Your focus now will have to be those children.'"

One dad recalled this heartwarming welcoming ceremony from his family for his new son:

> My family was ecstatic when Josh came. I went down that next weekend and, unbeknownst to me, my entire family had assembled. This was unprecedented—they all showed up all at one time, every single one of them. It was unprecedented; this only happened when we had weddings or funerals. I had no idea that they were all gathering, either. When I got there, they all ran out of the house, and my sister grabbed Josh, and he didn't know this woman—he was being passed from one person to another. It was a very nice thing; we had a lovely dinner and it was great.

On the other side, the parents of one gay dad completely rejected his decision to parent:

> My family has always been so nonsupportive of my life as a gay person, so it was no surprise when they were completely rejecting of my decision to parent. I told them that I planned to adopt, and they just rolled their eyes and said, "Do you really think that is fair to those children?" I have dealt with the pain I feel about their rejection of me, but in some small part of my heart I wished that they could have gotten over it and been there for my children as grandparents. I think I have reconciled this pain by realizing that my

family is missing so much by not being a part of Harlan and Jeremy's lives—they are such beautiful kids.

Whether they assumed that their parents would be supportive or not, a number of men reported that they did not consult their families in making their decision to parent:

> We didn't tell family, not until it came time; we discussed it a little bit with siblings beforehand but not parents. I felt like I was over thirty, thirty years old, and I felt like this was my personal decision, and they only needed to know as far as when it was more here. It was not something that I really cared for any input from people. It was between my partner and me, and other people didn't matter, except to be informed. I didn't feel like I needed approval from anyone. It was our decision. When we did tell our families, my family was fine, but Craig's family, especially his father, were very disapproving, so much so that they didn't meet our child until he was six months old. That was hard.

In fact, the parents of most of the men approved of their decision. Many were excited by the prospect of having a grandchild (one of the first laments from parents when a child comes out to them is that they had wanted grandchildren). Seeing their gay sons in this new role of daddy often brought gay men closer to their parents. They found new appreciation for and sensitivity to their parents' struggles to raise them, and they could rely on the support and guidance of their parents in raising their children. In a very real sense the narratives of the men interviewed suggest that no matter how different their parenting style was from their own parents', or how different the circumstances by which they became parents, their empathy for their parents increased when they stepped into the role of parent.

Finalization of the Adoption

The moment when a family becomes a family is not necessarily linked to the finalization of an adoption, but for some dads that

legal event created a feeling of closure, making them feel irrevo-
cably family. For one dad finalization meant no more agency intrusion in their lives:

> What I remember, when the adoption was finalized, [was]
> thinking, "Oh, good—I won't have these people in our lives
> anymore." Even if they were nice, there was always someone
> new coming to the door. And they could make a decision
> and change things. The first time I realized that they were
> going to be ours, I was so relieved that no one could take
> them from us and that they were finally ours, and that we
> didn't have to justify who we were or worry that if someone
> didn't like us, because we were gay or thought they should
> have a mom, or they only have two dads or whatever, that
> they could be taken from us.

Another dad was surprised by how much it mattered to him:
"Finalization was great, I didn't think it would be a big deal,
but it was. It is forever!"

The Challenges of Having Gay Parents

Children move through infancy, toddlerhood, preschool, school
age, and then adolescence, and the shifts and changes that parents
must weather as a child ages present numerous challenges for all
parents (Brazelton 1992; Gordon 2000; Larson and Richards 1994;
Wolf 2002). For the gay dads in this study, the most common issues they dealt with were (1) what do we tell them about their
families of birth? (2) how to handle the inevitable question of
where did I come from? (3) what to say when the child says, "I
wish I had a mom," and (4) growing up with gay parents.

What Do We Tell Them?/Where Do I Come From?

The majority of the men in this study were very comfortable talking with their children about their adoption, foster, or kinship
process. One dad's description of talking to his children about this
process captures all the elements mentioned by the other fathers:

We have always told them about their birth families and about how they were adopted. They love hearing the story of how we picked them up at the airport and how we brought them home. As they got older, they have had questions about their birth families, and we have told them as much as we know about them. We have also made it clear that we will help them to find their birth families when they are eighteen, if that is something that they want to do. I think we just kept our discussions very natural; every now and then I try to check in with them to just see how they are feeling about things, and their birth families is an area that we frequently talk about.

Dads in this study were clear that they needed to maintain open communication with their children about adoption, about their family configuration, and about gay-headed families. They also noted that most children were not that interested in communicating about these topics on a daily basis. Knowing when to address these issues and when not to talk about them was key. One dad described it this way:

> We try to weave things into the conversation normally, like when we are talking about our lives before we had children, we might say, "Before we adopted you . . ." Our oldest child thought for the longest time that being gay meant that you were in a committed relationship with another person of the same gender—it wasn't completely accurate, but we didn't go out of our way to correct him. Kids don't generally associate being gay with sex, but I think most children don't think of their parents as sexual beings. Sometimes we were, I think, overly sensitive about gay issues, and the kids would set us straight and let us know right away that whatever it was had nothing to do with their unique family situation.

These experiences seem to be corroborated by the work of H. David Kirk (1964) when he notes that adoptees handle adoption best when they are raised in families that allow them the freedom and opportunity to explore adoption-related issues (and, in this case, issues related to being in a gay-headed family) whenever they arise.

I Wish I Had a Mom

Most children live in worlds that are dominated by moms, not dads. Moms are highlighted in cartoons, on television commercials, and in videos and are usually the adults who bring younger children to school in the morning and pick them up in the afternoon. Although the majority of dads in this study did not seem to feel the need to intentionally connect their children with mother figures, they did acknowledge that their children sometimes verbalized a desire for a mother at one time or another. This desire took several forms, and the fathers were aware of what the verbalization for a mother meant for their own child. One dad recalls how his child expressed an interest in having a mother: "One day Wade just starting talk about his birth mom. It was near his birthday, and I think that often adopted kids think about their birth families during those anniversary times, but he just said, kind of sadly, 'I love you, Dad, but wish I had a mom.' I felt bad for him. I knew that there wasn't anything that I could do to make it better, but I just felt sad for him."

Other dads said that their child's lack of a mother was noted more by other children:

> My kids were obviously comfortable with their own family, but other kids, who were my children's friends, frequently mentioned about the lack of a mom in our family. In some cases the kids who were my children's friends were from single mom families or divorced families where they lived with their mom, with very little involvement with their dad, so the fact that our children had two dads was quite a different experience for them.

Children use parents in ways that make them feel safe and comfortable. One dad recalled how his son needed to be physically close to him and that he equated that need for closeness with a need for a mother figure: "Drew was a very tactile child. He needed, at times, to be close physically to me, and in times when he was very stressed he used to snuggle up close and say, 'I love to be all mushy with you—you are like a big fat mother pig.' He meant this as the highest compliment, and he clearly selected the mushier dad because my partner is the more physically fit of the two of us."

This dad suggests that his child had clearly thought about having a mom: "When I asked my son if he ever misses having a mom, he kind of looked at me incredulously and said, 'How can you miss something that you never had?'"

Growing Up with Gay Parents

During infancy and toddlerhood the issues of having a gay father are subtle and, for most children, irrelevant, because children are unaware of gender roles in the home (Goldman and Goldman 1983). The children of the men interviewed seemed to bond to their parent, and the parents were accepting of their children, praising them, correcting them when necessary, and creating a conscious environment of affection and warmth. Kirk, in his classic 1964 work on adoption, offers a perspective that may explain why the bond between adopted child and adoptive parent can be so strong, and I believe this also applies to these gay fathers and their children. According to Kirk's hypothesis, all have suffered a deep sense of loss: The gay dads experienced loss because of the exigencies associated with coming out as a gay man in a heterocentric and sexist world that presumes that they will never be a suitable primary parent; the children experience the loss of their birth families. When the parents understand the shared nature of their loss, they can be more empathic toward their child and better able to raise him or her in a sensitive and understanding way.

As the children of these twenty dads entered middle childhood (ages six through twelve), they began to further develop their sense of self (Brodzinsky, Schechter, and Marantz 1993), including the recognition of gender, racial, and cultural differences. These children also had to deal with differences in their family composition. Many issues brought to light by these dads seem to be related more to issues of adoption than to the parents' sexual orientation, but in some cases more subtle complexities are inextricably linked to adoption, foster care, and having a family that is considered different from the norm.

Brodzinsky, Schechter, and Marantz (1993) identify three milestones for children in this period of development that are related to adoption and that resonate with the experiences of these gay dads and their children. They are grieving for the lost family; beginning the search for birth family; and the pain of being different. Each of these themes was reflected in the interviews with the twenty fathers in this study, and although these factors may not have been directly linked to the sexual orientation of the fathers, they are an important aspect of the experience of fatherhood for these men.

Grieving for the Lost Family

Schoolage children begin to understand the implications that are inherent in not living with one's birth family. Many children start to feel a sense of loss for not being with their birth parents. Certainly this is true for children who are adopted as schoolage children or older, but even if children are adopted or fostered as infants, they still experience a sense of loss for their birth family and grieve for this loss. Many of the fathers interviewed noted this sense of loss in their children. Dave, a single dad with two children, reflected on this:

> My second child, Greg, is very verbal about grieving for his loss of his birth family, and I feel really bad, but I hardly have any information to share with him, either. This is a really different experience from his brother, Wade, who knows his birth mom and writes to her. Greg gets these tantrums at times and screams, "Even my real mom didn't want to take care of me and neither do you!" He just feels so worthless at these times, and I guess he cannot imagine that anyone could love him or be accepting of him. At these

times he is difficult to reach, but I just try to stay close by, and later, after he calms down, I try to spend some special time with just him. I notice that around the holidays and sometimes on his birthday, there also seems to be this sadness about him. I think it is also part of this grieving that he experiences.

I guess I will never know the loneliness that Greg feels, and it hurts that I cannot protect him from that—but I know that I can't.

Often, as Brodzinsky, Schechter, and Marantz (1993:71) note, adoptees don't even know why they feel so sad or so angry; the possibility that their feelings are related to grief is too abstract for them to grasp, and they suffer their emotions without being able to put a name on them.

Beginning the Search for Birth Family

Almost all adoptees search for their birth families. Why did I get adopted? What is my birth family really like? I wonder if they ever think about me? These are all questions that children who are separated from their families ask out loud or in the quiet privacy of self reflection. Such questioning usually begins during the early school years. Most of the gay dads in this study were very aware of the importance of the search process for their children. Mark, the father of a boy who was ten at the time of the interview, reflected on his son's yearning for his birth family:

> When Tom was about five, he started asking a lot of questions. I answered them when they came up and tried to check in with him every now and then to ask if he was wondering about his birth mom or his birth family. I always told him that we could try to find his mother when he became eighteen. One day, when I was going on a trip to the city where he knew that his birth family lived, he said, "Dad, can I come with you to Charleston?" I was caught off guard because I travel a lot for work, and he never had asked me before about coming with me, and I had forgotten that

this was the city where he was born. So I said, "Well, no, sweetie—you have to go to school and I have to work, but why do you want to come with me on this trip?" He looked at me with those beautiful innocent eyes, and he so innocently said, "Because I want to find my mommy." It was so sweet, so tender, it really broke my heart to see him . . . so earnest and thinking that we could find her in such a big city, but that's what makes kids so wonderful—they are so trusting and so hopeful. It made me so much more aware that even when he is not asking me directly about his birth family, in his own private little space he is thinking about conducting his search for them.

The Pain of Being Different

In middle childhood and then adolescence children become acutely aware of being different or being perceived as being different. Some children may relish their differentness, but most do not. Sometimes the children of these twenty men reported to their dads that they were teased in school for being adopted and for being the child of gay parents. Like the training that parents of color provide for their children to combat prejudice (Crumbley 1999), most of the gay men I interviewed spoke about providing their children with emotional armor against the pain of a taunt. But even with this emotional preparation by their dads, the children had to learn to protect themselves at school: "My eleven-year-old son, who struggles with being perceived as different and having a different kind of family, came home from school one day and said, 'You don't get it, do you? Do you know what they say to me in school? They say, "Like father, like son." 'You know, they make these cracks, trying to say that I'm gay, which I'm not, because you are.' It pisses me off!"

Another dad, who had become father to his niece, had a similar story:

One day Marisa came home from school crying and upset. When I asked what happened, she said that this one girl in

her school had a fight with her and yelled in front of everyone. "You don't even know your mother because she didn't
want you, and now you have to be taken care of by a faggot."
I tried to comfort her and said, "Okay, so the worst thing
that anyone could ever say to you now [has] happened, so
you don't have to worry about it happening anymore. Now
what do we do? Let's move forward."

As the children became teens, many of the dads found that they
had new issues to address in their families. Huge changes occur in
the years between thirteen and nineteen. Physically, teens grow at
a faster rate than at any time since the prenatal period (Marcia
1980; Offer 1969). Biological and emotional changes in adolescents strain most family systems (Wolf 2002). Most dads interviewed were clear that the changes that their child experienced
had less to do with their father's gay identity and more to do with
the emerging identity of the teenager (Wolf 2002). In some cases, however, the fathers did feel that their gay identity was at issue for their child. The comments of one father are representative
of many issues that the fathers discussed in regard to the changes
brought about by adolescent development:

> The onset of junior high school caused our son to deal with
> our family situation in different ways. While in grammar
> school all of his friends knew our family and had sleep-
> overs, spent time with us—our being gay was no big deal
> We knew their families, we socialized with their parents,
> and our gayness was a nonissue. However, when our son
> went to a new school, he had to meet new friends and
> make decisions about how much or how little he told them
> about his family. It was like the first day of camp but on a
> bigger scale. He now had the control over telling others
> about his gay dads, not us. It was sometimes difficult for
> him. But he learned to tell friends when he felt comfort-
> able, and he did not necessarily do that on day one. He also
> had to tell them he was adopted, and I think in some ways
> not having a mother was a bigger issue than having too
> many fathers.

As fathers of adolescent children, the gay dads in this study described how they had to learn a new set of rules about parenting. They had to get used to knocking on closed bedroom doors; they had to learn not to take adolescent moodiness personally; and they had to learn to let go. The hallmark of adolescence is moving toward independence, and for very involved parents such as the men in this study, allowing their child to move away from them was a necessary, but sometimes painful, process. Most of the dads acknowledged that this had less to do with them as gay men and more to do with the development of their teenage child. Nonetheless, caring for a teenage child was a new phenomenon for the men, and many were weighed down as well with memories of their own tumultuous adolescence. Some equated their own coming-out process as adolescents to the coming out that their children had to experience as the children of a gay parent: "Sometimes I felt guilty about giving him something else to deal with—having a gay father—in addition to being an already overburdened teenager. When you are the child of a gay parent, you always have to make decisions about whether or not to come out too. Whenever he meets new kids, he has to decide whether or not to tell them about his family. In addition, he also had to come out about being adopted and not having a mom. These are big issues for a teenager to deal with."

I emerged from compiling these accounts of the experiences of gay fathers with a sharpened sense of the diverse ways that they have created their families and in the process redefined fatherhood. As a consequence, these men's examples enrich our knowledge of fatherhood. This group of gay dads expands our capacity to explicate and portray the varied phenomena that occur within the institution of fatherhood as seldom before. In doing so, these unique fatherhood narratives dispel a powerful myth that men cannot nurture children and expand the typical, but narrowly defined, role of father as breadwinner. These narratives undermine other falsehoods as well, namely, that gay men cannot and should not be fathers and that gay people make inferior parents. A parallel inference that surfaces in exploring these gay dads' experiences is that heterocentrism, the privilege of heterosexual relations over gay identities, continues to complicate gay dads' efforts to be creative, resilient, and committed parents. The majority of men interviewed proved to be extraordinary parents to the children in their lives. In fact, the efforts that went into becoming a parent seem to have caused many to become very involved in and committed to their children's lives, perhaps more than the typical parent.

Creating a family is challenging, sometimes draining, sometimes joyful and consumes a great deal of energy. The process of parenthood changed the configuration of the lives of these men so that parenting came first. It was not an either-or choice (gay or dad) because each man is gay. But their focus, their energy, and their time went first into parenting and second into connecting with the gay world as members of the community.

Being a parent opened them up to a new world and gave their lives new meaning. But as I will explore in chapter 3, these dads had to do a lot of work and negotiating to change the communities in which they lived while growing into their role as father and social activist. Chapter 3 explores the issues of living in a family in a community context.

Three

Community Responses to Gay Dads

While waiting to check in at our hotel, on a very long line at Disney World, after a very long flight, I am confronted with the dreaded question from a stranger: "Who's the dad, you or the dark-haired guy?" "We both are" is my usual pat response.

"I don't get it," replies the stranger. "Are your children adopted?"

"Yes," I respond, "and we are a family, all four of us." "I don't get it," she says again.

"What don't you get?" I respond a bit testily.

"How could two men and two kids be a family?" she replies without having any idea of what she is getting into.

"We are a gay couple, and we adopted the boys when they were infants. This is our family—now do you get it?"

Her puzzled expression quickly changes into the un-mistakable recognition of "Oh, now I get it, but you did-n't have to tell me you were gay, I didn't want to know that." Even other people on the line have a reaction, as they are listening in on our conversation.

> I think, "What a hassle, what a drag, to have to explain
> our family to complete strangers, who probably mean no
> harm but are nonetheless intrusive into a private matter
> that a heterosexual couple would never have to ad-
> dress."
>
> —Mark, a forty-five-year-old gay father

A gay man who has children discovers early on that the delicate question of when and why and to whom to come out is no longer in his control. For all the gay men in this study the issue of coming out itself was not new. They had each, in their adult lives, learned to gauge situations to determine whether to come out or pass as straight. They had experienced the luxury of having control over the process, at least most of the time. But once they had children, they learned that they were being outed all the time, every day, to complete strangers who asked nosy questions, to parents of other children, to school officials, the crossing guard, the playground attendant, the doctor's staff, the dentist's staff, the checkout clerk at the grocery store—in short, to everyone who wondered aloud, "Who is that child to you? And where is her mother?"

When I asked the fathers to rate themselves on a scale of 1 to 10, with 10 being the most out, the vast majority (85 percent) rated themselves at 9. Clearly, these men were comfortable with their gay identity. Most had been out for an average of fifteen years. They had ample experience negotiating supportive, indifferent, and hostile responses to their disclosure. Yet they all remarked on how fatherhood entailed a nearly constant state of self-declaration to the community at large.

Out in the Community

Although being open about their sexual orientation ostensibly benefited these men, being out as a gay dad in the social community was, as I will explore in this chapter, another issue entirely. The social world of children involves, as the gay men interviewed for this study noted, traveling into heterosexual territory. Suddenly, gay dads were sharing the common identity of parent with a large group of nongay people and found themselves coming out to acquaintances and trying to help them understand that gay men could be and in fact were fathers. Many men shared anecdotes about being put on the spot by well-meaning but intrusive questions. The query might come from other parents at the child's school or parents of other toddlers at the playground or the person giving the child his or her first hair cut or the photographer snapping the family's holiday portrait at Sears. Gay dads encountered many awkward moments that forced them to discuss the intimate fact of their sexual orientation, essentially with complete strangers. One father summed up what he felt was the relinquishment of his privacy:

> When you are a parent, especially as the kids get older and start to socialize with other children, you are thrust into a new world of straight people who happen to be parents. Almost immediately, at the playground or at the pediatrician's office, you are confronted with people who you do not know very well, asking you very personal questions. Our very presence at the playground engenders this inquisitiveness because it is so seldom that men are seen with young children, particularly infants.
>
> I don't always feel like disclosing this to them, but somehow there is a level of intimacy and sharing that happens between parents, and usually I just tell them when they start asking those questions that I am a gay dad. My own personal decision about privacy is outweighed by my desire to model honesty, openness, and pride for my child. I guess I don't really have to come out to them, and sometimes I don't right away, but it just makes things easier right away from the beginning. It's not a political statement—it's not who I am totally, but as a gay dad, I just don't fit into the preconceived notions that people on the playground have of men with small children.

Because they had been out for more than a decade, most of the gay dads understood the risks that they were taking for themselves and their family when they came out. Even living in large urban areas with gay populations was no guarantee that the person to whom they were coming would not react with fear, aversion, distaste, or outright anger and hatred toward them for being gay, or with moral objections that a gay man or gay couple was raising a child. These negative feelings might range from questioning a gay man's ability or appropriateness as a parent to expressions of overt hostility. The stress of being on guard against such assaults put several men on the offensive. This posturing was a phenomenon that several discussed in interviews and may be a reason for the overcompensation issues discussed in chapter 2. One dad described it this way:

> It was always easier to just come out, because the stress of not telling them was worse. But in the back of my mind I always felt scared that, much as I liked this person and much as I wanted our kids to be friends, suppose she really got weird on me and started to distance herself and her child from us? What if no one ever talked to us, what if no one wanted to play with my child because of me?
>
> I know this sounds crazy, but these were my fears initially. It was all right with me if they didn't like me, but I didn't want them to dislike my child because of me. You know, to tell you the truth, in my experience my fears were never realized—it never happened—but the stress of worrying about it, at least initially, when Josh was younger, was a real burden for me.

Coming out as a gay person, whether as a dad or not, is fraught with very real danger. The men felt many of the same emotions that they experienced when they came out before being parents: fear of rejection, fear of judgment, fear of negative repercussions in their work lives, fear of danger to their physical safety. But the key difference that they articulated about coming out as a gay dad was their awareness that they were also outing their child as being a member of a gay family and that their child might also be rejected or judged or teased or stigmatized. In most cases, however, these fears did not prove true; nonetheless, the anxiety of pending disclosure was stressful to the men interviewed and added another dimension to the usual strain and fatigue of parenthood.

Despite the possibility of negative responses, the gay dads had no shortage of parents who welcomed them, supported them, and shared their lives with them. Although other gay dads were a strong source of support, all the men interviewed found acceptance from colleagues at work, neighbors, and heterosexual parents of their children's friends, as well as from teachers, pediatricians, and religious institutions. One dad's comments summed up what many of the men told me:

> Our life is so completely different now that Max is eight years old from what I first imagined it would be like when he was an infant. Although we are still connected to gay friends, most of our friends are people both gay and not gay, single or coupled, who have children. Now it's children, not being gay, that is the common denominator in our relationships. It was so weird for us at first to be so involved with straight couples. I mean, without our children, we would have nothing in common with these folks, but they are really great people for the most part. I remember being so afraid at first that they wouldn't like us or our child, but I can't think of one case where we lost a friend or didn't become close to a family because we were gay. Our being gay didn't really matter—we were all parents [and] that is what mattered.

Several strong themes emerged from interviews with the gay dads about community responses to their parenting. All the men, without exception, noted that their relationship to the community at large was transformed, and in many ways expanded, because of their role as parents, more specifically, because of their children.

The Day-to-Day Reality of Parenting in a Community

> I can't find my sneakers, do you know where are my sneakers are?
> There's no milk for my cereal—

I forgot to tell you I have a class trip today—
I need a shoe box for my science project.
I don't feel so good, I don't think I can go to school.

Seldom does the day-to-day conversation in a gay-headed family focus on anything that remotely has to do with the gay identity of the parent. The complete irrelevance of the parent's sexual identity in day-to-day parenting routines was a phenomenon that the gay fathers noted frequently. One dad summarized his experiences this way:

> My life as a parent is very similar to the lives of other people who are parents. Being gay or not has almost nothing to do with it. I laugh when people think that gay people have these wild exotic lives, dancing in discos, going to parties, having a fabulously decorated apartment. Maybe some single gay people have that kind of life, but gay people who are parents definitely have a very different experience. It's very routine. We get up, we get ourselves ready for the day, we get the kids off to school, and we get ourselves to work. If one kid is sick, we have to decide who is going to stay home this time and who absolutely cannot. This usually depends on who has a meeting and who doesn't. We get to work, we run home from work to pick the kids up from school, do homework, maybe play for an hour, make dinner, watch a video, get baths, lay out clothes for the next day, read them a story, get them into bed, maybe do laundry or something that is relaxing and adultlike after they are asleep. And if we don't fall asleep with them first as we are putting them to bed, then we crash into bed ourselves. Exciting, huh?

Most of the dads said it was absurd to be regarded as extraordinary for doing something so ordinary. The ordinariness of parenting, and the common tasks that all parents share in raising children, seemed far removed from gay lifestyle or gay identity issues, yet the fathers lived with the dissonance of having their seemingly ordinary family viewed as a curiosity by the outside world, both gay and nongay.

In some ways, you become even more separated from the gay community as you become a parent. The world of parents doesn't involve a lot of the aspects of life that single gay men enjoy. In fact, to be a good parent many of the qualities you need are to be routine, steady, and, yes, boring! If you are still leading a fabulous, exciting life and you are a parent, chances are you're not spending much time being a good parent, because being a good parent means spending a great deal of time and energy with your children—at least that's my definition of good parenting.

Neighborhood Issues

Unlike inquisitive strangers who want gay dads to explain themselves, neighbors are people with whom gay families have ongoing contact, although not necessarily a high level of intimacy. Neighbors get to know one another over time and engage in various levels of conversation about shared issues such as crime, garbage pickup, mail delivery, or traffic—whatever is affecting their mutual environment. They have some knowledge of the details of one another's lives. Some gay dads were clear that neighbors had distinctly different reactions to their choice to parent and that these reactions varied by geographic location. One dad in an urban neighborhood made this comment:

> In Midville everyone was very supportive; everyone knew I was gay. When I moved there, I immediately got involved with the neighborhood. I got involved with the block association, I became the president, [and] we transformed the block. We got the Most Beautiful Block in Brooklyn [award] four years in a row. Then I became involved with the community board so I was deeply involved, and I think they were used to me being different. When Josh came, they just said, "Oh, that gay man down there, he adopted a child." They were always giving advice, telling me what I should do. When we moved to Manhattan, there were just so many gay people in our building, so it was not a big

thing. I got involved organizing events and playgrounds for
kids in our building. Being gay was no issue.

Another dad agreed about the need to find a neighborhood that
would be a good fit for his family:

> We intentionally moved to our neighborhood because we
> had researched it and knew that it had a great school district
> and it was friendly and open to gay people. We were also in-
> terested in the fact that it is a very diverse community. I
> guess, given that we are also within the city limits, the fact
> that we are an urban environment was also an important fac-
> tor for us. It seems that folks are less judgmental in an ur-
> ban environment; most people in the city don't care what
> you do, and for us that worked.

Another dad talked about how he and his partner participated
in community events and didn't worry about whether neighbors
were open to them or not: "We live in a very conservative area of
California; we have never had people be not accepting, at least not
to our faces. We made a very conscious choice to participate in the
community. We purposely made the monster not big. We have
been very involved, and people know who we are."

Although the subjects for the study predominately lived in urban centers, several lived in the suburbs of New York and Los Angeles. The fathers in those gay-headed families reported a range of
experiences, from positive welcoming communities to hostile and
dismissive ones. One dad was unpleasantly surprised to find that
moving his family to the suburbs was a difficult adjustment because of the negative responses of their neighbors to having gays
move in down the block:

> The house was wonderful, the yard was wonderful the built-
> in pool was wonderful.
>
> Generally, the neighbors were not wonderful. There were
> a couple of neighbors who were very offensive. For me it was
> truly hateful to live in the suburbs because I commuted
> everyday and that added about two and one half hours on to
> my already long workday. I would drop the baby off at sev-

en A.M. for preschool, and then my partner picked him up at five. I would get home just in time to go to bed and then get up at six A.M. and do it all over again. Moving to the suburbs was something I said I would never do and something that I never should have done.

It was even more difficult with my partner because he was isolated, very isolated, up there and had almost no friends. It created an additional strain at work also because if there were problems there, I couldn't just pop right in or hop in a cab and be on my way to work, so there were lots of problem. It was not a healthy time for our family. It was great having all that space with the kids, but we just never felt settled in that house. It was not a healthy situation.

The neighbors directly behind our house hated us because we were gay. They were very clear that it was because we were gay and that's about it. They said that our gay identity flew in the face of their religious principles. The neighbors across the street hated us because we were gay and because we had children, whom they felt we had no business having. The neighbors on another corner to our backyard hated us because we were gay and because the children were not white. The neighbor across the street continues to be a very good friend of mine to this day. Clearly, this wasn't an accepting neighborhood. But we also didn't fulfill their fantasies of what gay people were supposed to be like—as one neighbor said to me, "You're just as boring as the rest of us." We lived there for five years [and] it was a horrible experience for us. When we moved back to the city, it was such a big relief!

One interesting issue that hostile male neighbors raised was related to the threat to their patriarchal privileges from the presence of gay men who were blatantly taking on traditionally female responsibilities in the home:

One neighbor said to me, "You've made life very difficult for the husbands in the neighborhood, because all wives want the husbands to take care of the house, take care of the yard, take good care of the kids, take them to the grocery shop, and all of the other things that they see you guys doing." They figured [if] we could do it and we were men, then why couldn't their husbands share in some of the responsibilities of raising children and caring for the house? In general, the women were much more accepting than the men. Frequently, when their husbands were not at home, the women would sneak over to talk with us and even hang out for a while. The husbands, however, were generally very hostile and never had anything to do with us.

A single dad, who also lived with his two sons in a suburb, recounted a very different experience:

We didn't move into our community. I lived in that house for many years before I had the children, so I didn't move into the neighborhood with my children, and that makes a difference. I was already there, pretty well established, had a business, knew a lot of people, and people liked me before they found out that either I was gay or that I was a gay dad. They just liked me previous to that. So I haven't witnessed any kind of hostility or changes in their attitudes toward me once I had children. I often wonder, though, if it would have been different if I had a partner. They see me as "single dad with children"; I am not sure they always think "single gay dad with children." But in reality, in our community there were gay people everywhere—this kid on Wade's basketball team, his uncle was gay and had a florist business with his partner. This other kid on the basketball team also had an uncle who was also gay who would come to his games. One of the parents in the play group had a sister and a brother who were both gay. I always tried to make sure that [the children] knew that gay people are all around us, not just their dad. But we started out with the neighborhood, and feeling comfortable being a gay dad in the neighborhood was no big deal, even if we were in the suburbs. There was a lot of diversity in the community. We just sort of grew into being a family there very comfortably.

Race/Cultural Issues

The majority—75 percent—of the twenty gay dads in this study
were caucasian and 15 percent were African American; 10 percent
were Latino. But 91 percent of the children of the gay dads were
kids of color, 62 percent Latino and 29 percent African American.
Raising a child from another race or culture presents adoptive
parents with significant challenges (Crumbley and Little 1997;
Lancaster 1996:82; McRoy, Oglesby, and Grape 1997; McRoy
and Zurcher 1983; Melina 1998:209). The parent who chooses to
raise a child of color, as many of these men remarked, has to develop a conscious awareness of what it means to be a person of col-
or in a predominately caucasian society. Dads who were of the
same culture or race as their children also felt a responsibility to
educate their children about what it meant to be a person of col-
or in a predominately white-skinned society. One dad described
the cultural differences very directly: "A black child raised in a
white family has to be able to deal with many challenges. Many
men feel that they can be colorblind, but that is just bullshit—
it's more than that."

A caucasian dad identified what he felt was the ideal situation
for transracial adoption: "Raising a black child in a white home is
an issue. In an ideal world same-race adoptions work out best for
children, but it is not an ideal world. The reality for these children was [that] they needed a permanent family who love them
and where they could be placed together. At my family events,
given that Paul is black and we are mostly a caucasian family, I
was conscious about how much Paul stood out."

Most dads were very much aware of the complexities that they
and their children faced as they confronted a world that is still
largely unaccustomed to transracial families:

> Well, we bring much more consciousness of diversity, and,
> I mean, I definitely see that in our kids. And as they get old-
> er, I see that they're going to be these incredible, well-
> rounded, confident, accepting kind of people that are going
> to be in interesting relationships because there's a sensitivi-
> ty to a lot of different issues. It just seems like our kids are

more sensitive to difference of all sorts. So it would be interesting to see, do they get into a situation where they're in a relationship where the woman makes all the money and they parent? Or do they become single parents themselves? I would think they will want to become parents, although maybe they could also decide not to parent.

Raising a black child in a black home had a deep significance to the dads in those families:

> I guess we kind of naturally address the issues of race all the time. As a black man, and a gay black man, I have grown up to be attuned to discrimination and prejudice. I think it is part of my job as a parent to prepare my children for what they will face in a predominately caucasian world, both good things and bad things. I don't think we focus exclusively on being black. It's obvious that we are, and I guess what I try to do more is to, consciously, to expose them to people of all races. In this city, that isn't very hard to do. It is also one of the reasons why the city is such a great place to raise children. In African American families there are a lot of different kinds of families. In my neighborhood where I grew up there were lots of children growing up without mom-and-dad families. I think that, being black, I have instilled in them that at some level it is important to be sensitive to issues about people of color. I think my kids are from a generation, however, where color is less of an issue for them and also it is about living in New York City and about social class as well.

The two Latino fathers who participated in the study were raising children in the context of kinship care. Because they shared the same racial and family heritage, cultural differences between father and children were not an issue. They did, however, feel a responsibility for passing on cultural traditions to their children:

> We don't focus too much on the fact that we are Latinos. We are of the same family, so there are a lot of similarities. I think what I try to pass on to them is two things: one—

the traditions of our family, especially around holiday issues, and, second, I try to help them see that there are people in the world who don't like us because we are Latinos.
This is the job of all parents, right? To teach their children
the ways of their family and to help protect them from potential harm by people who may not understand or appreci-
ate our culture and traditions.

Although all the dads in the study expressed a consciousness
about racial and cultural differences within the family, they had
varying levels of sensitivity to the issue. Some dads acknowledged
that they did not dwell on the topic as much as some of their
friends who had also adopted transracially or transculturally.
These fathers acknowledged that they spent more time talking to
their children about other differences, such as being adopted or
growing up without a mom in the family.

As far as ethnic heritage goes, people said to me all the time,
"Oh, try and learn Spanish and teach them Hispanic heritage," and I have really done next to nothing about it. I
mean, we eat in Mexican restaurants, and, I mean, I would
talk about the Mexican Revolution, but I don't do much on
that end. Some people feel really strongly about instilling
the native culture in their children. I have some friends with
Russian kids, and they learned about Russian heritage and
bought Russian clothes and go into more detail than I do. I
felt strongly about being out as far as being gay—I never
hid that and had a family, and I felt strongly about us being
an adopted family, I mean, it was obvious. We don't look
alike or whatever, but once in a while, when they were little, some stranger would come up to us in a public place and
say something like, "You must have a gorgeous Hispanic
wife." "Nope! No wife, they're adopted." That's what I'd always say! So there are certain areas that I felt strongly that
needed to be always talked about openly and honestly. I
think keeping dialogue open about their moms is much
more important for them. My youngest son just asked me
last night; he said, "What was my birth mother's name for

me if she decided to keep me?" I said, "I have no idea—I think she made the adoption plan all along so she probably didn't think about naming you." I always try to keep it open. I try to bring it up nonchalantly once a month, regularly, just like, "Oh, your eyes are gorgeous, you have your birth mother's eyes"—just like that, so they know it's a comfortable thing to talk about it.

Racism exists in all sectors of society, and even well-intentioned individuals still harbor racist beliefs and preconceptions. This was true of some extended family members of the gay dads who adopted transracially. Although they voiced support for the gay dad, these relatives sometimes made racist comments. "When I said that I was going to adopt a black child," one father recalls, "one relative said I should get an Asian child instead because they did better on tests."

School

Beginning with day care, schools are the most important and influential external system that shape and socially mold children's lives. School is the first place where children have to learn to negotiate without their parent's being physically present to intervene. Schools are also significant transmitters of heterocentric norms and mainstream culture. Most gay dads in this study were very involved in the selection of their children's schools and had a high level of involvement and interaction with teachers and administrators. Every single father was actively involved with the Parent-Teacher Association at their children's school or served as a class parent and was an active volunteer for all school-related events.

You start to ask the things of other parents, you just start asking immediately, "Where is there a good preschool?" Then you go and interview them and choose the one you like. Usually people in the neighborhood all send their kids to the one or two preschools that they like and that they can afford. I didn't go into any place identified as a gay active parent. I just went into the school and said, "I'm a parent and I am looking for a good program for my child." As far as I was concerned, I just wasn't going to deal with all of the issues up front. They were there—certainly they were there—but basically I never wanted to be identified as a gay. I just wanted to be known because of who I am, as an active involved parent. For me, for example, a lot of that was my being involved in the school; physically, I was there a lot, and so the kids and the schools and the parents knew us. That probably helped somewhat to get over the barrier because I was there and I was just as boring as the rest of the parents, all involved with my child's life—you get the same concerns as any other parent. We wanted a school where our child would be safe, welcomed, and could learn. It wasn't about us; it was about what was right for them.

Another dad had a different take on his initial engagement with the school system:

One of my great teachers was Fran Goshen [pseudonym for a well-known teacher], who told me that we had to tell the preschool teacher that we were gay. I mean, sometimes I dropped off Josh and sometimes Mark did, so they knew both of us. We had a parent-teacher conference, and we told the teacher that one of the reasons we wanted to meet you was that we wanted to tell you about our family so that you will really understand this: We are gay and we are raising Josh, and we didn't tell you before because we weren't clear how the school would respond. And she said, "I am so glad that you told me because I have been waiting to talk to you about that, but I didn't know how to talk to you." . . . What happened was that on Monday, when she asked Josh how his weekend was, he said that he had a great weekend because he got to sleep in bed with Daddy and Poppy—so unbeknownst to us, Josh had already outed us; everyone . . . already knew this. This was an eye-opening experience. Fran was right on—you have to tell them, because if you don't, your kids will tell them. It is also safer and healthier to tell yourself.

The majority of the men interviewed did feel that it was important to be proactive and to talk with the teachers about their different-looking families. Some mentioned that school personnel seemed generally uncomfortable discussing such issues as gay-parented families and children who are being raised without a mother:

> When Andrew first went to the school, we decided to meet with his teacher and talk with her about our family. When we met and said, "We wanted to let you know about our family situation," she quickly interjected and said, "Oh, we received training on that, and we have had other gay families in the school so it's not an issue for us." It wasn't an issue for us, either, but her discomfort with the topic kind of took us by surprise. It was like she didn't want to talk about it at all. Nonetheless, she was always great with our child, and that was really the issue, not us.

Parents also felt strongly that their children should not feel marginalized because their dads were gay, but they also pointed to two other issues that their children frequently had to address:

> Although we were clear that school was about the child, not us, we were concerned about the fact that so much of what is discussed in schools is so heterocentric. It's all about moms and dads. We wanted to make sure that the school was conscious about the many different kinds of families that children came from. In the case of our children, it was really more about the absence of a mom in our household, and also about adoption, rather than about being gay. I think it has been more difficult for our kids to answer questions like "where's your mom?" Or "how come you don't have a mom?" They also hear, "How come you were adopted?" Or, "Why didn't your real family want you?" Those are much more difficult questions for kids to deal with. Kids, especially younger children, don't pay much attention to the gay issue.

The process of handling school issues changed for the gay dads when their second child entered the school system: "With our second child, there was no such discussion, because they already knew us. We were in the PTA, we had been class parents, we were very active in the school, and everyone knew us."

As children grew up, some of the men found that the need for disclosure to school personnel about their sexual orientation began to seem less compulsory:: "When Andrew went to junior high, there was no need for us to meet with teachers about our family, even though it was a new school for him. In junior high kids [are] much more independent and are on their own; they no longer need or want their parents to run any kind of interference for them."

During the high school years, according to the fathers, they found little need for parental disclosure or involvement in the schools:

> As our children become teenagers, they need us less and less to intervene. Our oldest child, who is fifteen, is always saying, "Don't talk to me at the school concert, just meet me outside after it's over." At first, if you don't understand teens, you could think, "This is because we're gay," but it's not—it's what all teenagers are telling their parents. We meet with teachers if they have parent-teacher conferences, but it is amazing how different these first meetings are than when he first started school as a preschooler. Now we're worried about his geometry grades, not about whether or not they are sensitive to the uniqueness of his family situation.

Health Care Providers

Finding a good pediatrician to care for one's child is one of the most important factors in good parenting (Brazelton 1992:451). As they had in finding a good school, many dads relied on the recommendations of their friends, family members, and other parents. Once again, the fathers had to decide how much to tell their child's doctor:

> My partner's sister, who had a daughter, told us about her pediatrician, and then we moved from Midville, Brooklyn, to Manhattan, and we changed to another pediatrician who

she also recommended. He was very gay friendly; he actually was very, very supportive. His wife was a best friend with the head of Center Kids. At first I didn't come out, and he would ask kind of leading questions, and I was vague because I wasn't completely out. Then I told him we are gay, and he was absolutely fine about it. When we were doing this at first, we didn't know what we were doing. We didn't know how we were supposed to introduce these situations to people, how you were supposed to respond. It was always a learning experience.

Another dad was much more direct in his approach with potential pediatricians for his child: "When I first brought Wade to the pediatrician, I interviewed the pediatrician and I told him that I adopted him, that he was Hispanic, and that I was a single gay dad."

Other dads found that health care professionals had a hard time trusting the fathers' instincts, judgment, and ability to care for a young child simply because they were men:

> I remember one time it was a group practice, and I called the nurse, saying, "You know, Wade has a fever, what should I do now?" And she said, "Why don't you put your wife on?" and I said, "There is none—I'm it," and she said, "Oh, you must be Doctor Marsh's patient." So, obviously, I was the only single dad in that enormous practice, and I mean there were like five doctors in the practice—you know what I mean—so it was kind of telling: "Oh, you must be Doctor Marsh's patient." So I went in and I remember at the time I was fuming—I was so pissed off—and I thought, "How dare she ask that [to speak to his wife]" I'm the parent.

The legal issues of which partner is the real (i.e., legal) dad, which often smoldered on the back burner for gay coparents, became very real when a child had a medical emergency:

> When Drew fell and we had to rush him to the hospital, we were really scared, I mean, our kid was bleeding and we were a mess. When we ran into the emergency room, the first thing we were confronted with was, "Which one of you

is the dad?" Legally, my partner was the parent, so, right then and there, even in this emergency situation, and even though I was holding Drew, I had to back off and let my partner take charge because of his legal status. It was so upsetting to me and to Drew too.

Health insurance coverage was also a clear reminder of disparities in legal status:

> Going to the doctor or the dentist, at least at first, until they knew me, was always so annoying. The kids have my partner's last name, not mine, and they are on his health care insurance policy, but I was the one bringing them to the doctor. There were always a bunch of intrusive questions. Sometimes I got so tired of telling people our personal family business—usually they were very nice, but that first encounter was always such an invasion of our privacy.

Recreation Issues

Helping children to socialize through play is one of the hallmarks of parenting (Brazelton 1992:208). Setting up play dates for toddlers was a novelty for the first-time dads. And they had to learn that as children get older, their play needs also change:

> As Mack changed from baby to toddler, we wondered how he would develop. The play date thing was easy—we made friends with some of the moms and set up a time for our kids to play. But, as he grew, his athletic abilities were in direct contrast with our own. We were always the last picked for sports and dreaded gym class. Bill spent his childhood lip-syncing to Judy Garland records [and] now we are raising a jock. People went out of their way to say that Mack was one hundred percent boy, but once in a while he threw us a curve ball, like when he decided to paint his nails. When he did this, we of course thought it was about us, not him, but now we realize how wrong we were—he was just being himself. Some of our issues were just internalized homophobia.

Because many of the gay dads were very involved in the lives of their children, their homes were frequently the meeting places for other neighborhood children. Opening their homes to the friends of their children seemed to be a hallmark of gay dads' parenting styles in this study. They often played host to other people's children, which created an interesting set of dynamics.

> We have a sleepover almost every weekend. There are as many as eight or ten kids here on any given afternoon during the week. Since we have a pool, the entire neighborhood seems like they are here in the summer. I love having our home open to our kids and their friends. There is another benefit also with all of these kids here all the time: You really get to meet their parents also—so frequently, there are lots of parents here too. Someone once asked me if the other parents seemed afraid to let their children come over to our house because we were gay. Are you kidding? I wish some of them were afraid—their kids are here more than they are at their own homes.

Many dads also noted how their attitudes toward play changed once they actually had children, as this father suggests:

> I remember when we first had kids, we swore that we would never let our kids have toy guns. Now our playroom looks like an arsenal—you just can't stop them. If you refuse to buy them guns, they turn sticks into guns. Our biggest dilemma initially was, are they really going to get the living room messy and were we going to be able to deal with it? Well, they do get it really messy, and we are not bothered by it. Lots of things change when you become a parent, and you need to know when to hold firm and when to be flexible.

Integration into the Community

Four overarching themes emerged from the interviews with the dads. The first two include issues around adoption, as well as caring for children who are not biologically related to the father (Lancaster 1996:68; Melina 1998:83). The third theme relates directly to issues of gay male sexual orientation and what I call mothercentric practice. The final theme relates to the need for gay dads to reframe their relationship to the gay community.

Oh, They're Adopted—What Lucky Children!

Many of the men interviewed noted how the general public is sometimes ignorant of the adoption and foster care process (Brodzinsky, Schechter, and Marantz 1993; Lancaster 1996; Melina 1998). Several fathers noted that questions about adoption and acclamations about their selflessness were unsettling and disconcerting. One father expressed the sentiments of many other men in the study:

> Sometimes people just strike up this conversation with you about the adoption process, and then they start asking very inappropriate questions in front of the children. This one woman starting asking me how much I paid for them, and did I know their mothers—right in front of the kids without any regard for their feelings or for how inappropriate her questions were. I was so angry. The one comment, however, that really gets to me the most is [that] these children are so lucky to be adopted! I know that people who say that mean it as a compliment, but it isn't, and they are not lucky: I am lucky to have these beautiful children in my life and to have the opportunity to be part of their lives.

Is He Your Real Child?

Several men interviewed said that strangers and acquaintances often challenged the validity of their parenthood by making insensitive or unkind comments to suggest that adoption or foster care is a second-class form of parenthood. Brodzinsky, Schechter, and Marantz (1993:30) note that this question, albeit unpleasant, is not an uncommon one for adoptive parents. Lancaster (1996:68–73) goes one step further in offering advice to adoptive parents about how to respond proactively to such remarks. Lancaster's suggestion, to approach the insensitivity of these questions head-on and to point out their hurtfulness, can be useful advice to adoptive parents dealing with this issue. One dad's comment was representative: "Nothing makes me angrier than when someone says, 'Oh, they're adopted—I thought they were your real children.' As if having my children biologically would make them any more real or important to me. It's really hurtful when people say things about my children. People are so insensitive sometimes."

Integration in the Gay Community

For the men in the study, becoming a parent meant having to reframe their role in the gay community. Although many dads initially felt estranged from the single gay community, they found a new sense of community with a group of other parents who are gay and lesbian.

> After being so totally isolated from the gay community, which I had been so enmeshed in, which I now see as the gay single community—I have found a whole new group of gay men who are dads. I have also become close with a number of lesbian moms. I don't think I would have typically become friends with these folks, but, once again, it's the children that brought us together. As gay parents, we have a great camaraderie with one another. It's a very important support group for me.

But this same gay dad drew important distinctions between gay men who are parents and heterosexual fathers:

> In the straight community with straight dads, I have more camaraderie with the moms in the straight community than with the dads. In the straight world, with few exceptions, dads are not actively involved in the parenting process. Because we're parenting and we're all parenting full time, I have more in common with the straight moms than the straight dads. If a dad is commuting to the city to New York and goes to New York on the seven o'clock train and

comes home on the seven o'clock at night train, then he is a
weekend dad; [he] is not really involved as the primary parent. You can't be a primary parent and work twelve hours a
day. It's just not possible. The wife's doing the parenting
and staying home from work for the kid's sake and making
the phone calls and arranging the play dates and going to
the birthday parties and keeping the calendar and doing all
those things.

Where's the Mother?

The one subject that all the dads discussed at length was the multitude of questions from people in the community about their
child's mother or lack thereof.

The initial stuff about where is the mother always comes up
with people you just meet. Then there are several other
questions that come up: "What do you mean there are no
moms in your family?" "Don't you think that children really need a mom?" "Don't you think your children need a
mother figure in their lives?" There is an assumption that
children are being neglected by not having a female role
model. The assumption is based on the mistaken belief that
for some reason that men cannot be adequate primary parents. Society says that women are supposed to raise children,
not men. Men are supposed to have a bigger impact on children when they are teenagers. There is also this assumption
that our children live in a bubble and that they will grow up
not being able to know about or to deal with women. My
kids are very connected to women; they have aunts, they
have grandmothers, their teachers are women, their babysitter is a woman, they have a lot of opportunities to interact
with women. Sometimes, I think they might need a mother, but our family consists of two men parenting two children; there isn't much that we can do about that at this
point. The funny thing is, most of our children's friends
have one mom and no dads in their lives. So, in a way, our

kids are exposed to dads in a way that their friends are not.
A lot of this has changed over the years, but the issues about
mothers come up frequently.

> By the fact that we are gay with children, we are already
> activists. Every action we participate in, going to the mall,
> to church, to the doctor, we are out as gay people. Our
> children have to educate people also.

As men in nurturing roles, as primary parents in a society that
typically does not view males in this role, gay dads are, just by
virtue of their existence, radical parent activists, whether they
want to be or not. Gay men in straight communities have learned
to engage school and health care systems, and the personnel who
run them, to access services and an appropriate educational experience for their children. Gay dads, initially distanced from the
single gay world, found new community with heterosexual parents and with other gay and lesbian parents.

> I think the best thing is just watching life unfold and open-
> ly hav[ing] a hand in it, and hop[ing] that it's unfolding
> well. I think that's probably absolutely the best thing to
> find and watch a human bond and become something better
> and something more. I love watching my two kids interact
> independently with me, even when they don't know I'm
> watching. I feel so truly blessed to be a parent and to be a
> part of my children's lives. I can't think of anything else
> worth more than that!

Four

Gender Politics and Gay Male Parenthood

Implications for Practice

> We're halfway there. We've begun to raise our daughters more like sons so now, women are whole people. But fewer of us have the courage to raise our sons more like daughters. Yet until men raise children as much as women do and are raised to raise children, whether or not [they] become fathers they will have a far harder time developing in themselves those human qualities that are wrongly called "feminine" but are really those necessary to raise children: empathy, flexibility, patience, compassion, and the ability to let go.
>
> —*Gloria Steinem, Smith College commencement address, 1993*

The feminist revolution of the past forty years has challenged centuries of presuppositions about what men and women are naturally suited to do and be. The phenomenon of gay men who choose to become fathers can be seen in the context of the feminist transformation of modern U.S. society: These men, who once would not have considered themselves capable of being a primary parent to a young child, or even entitled to be a father, were suddenly open to thinking about expanded options for their lives, options that included children. Perhaps because they had already challenged the patriarchy's heterosexism—the assumption that all normal people are heterosexual—the idea could occur to them to pursue such a radical path as parenthood.

When I began this research, I had specific ideas about gay men choosing to be parents; these notions were shaped by my exposure to academic, media, cultural, and personal discourses. After interviewing gay men who had chosen to become parents, I returned to my initial questions: What made these gay men become parents? How did these men change as a result of becoming parents, and how are they changing the institution of parenthood as we know it? What are some of the implications for social work practice and, specifically, for child welfare practice with respect to gay men who choose to be parents?

Sexism and Parenthood

In many subtle and complex ways the politics of gender, rather than sexual orientation, were the main theme of the interviews with the gay dads. What I mean by the politics of gender is really sexism, that is, the basing of social and personal expectations and opportunities not on talent, proclivity, or desire but simply on gender. (Transgender, I would add, is still so invisible in our society that it is not even part of the conversation about gender politics). Sexism affected the gay dads at almost every stage of their journey to parenthood and continues to be a factor even now.

The theme of sexism seemed to branch in four directions: questions of voice and choice; how gay fatherhood expands our definition of parenthood; how gay dads challenge traditional (patriarchal) roles for males; and the way gay fathers struggle to find recognition and validation as they take on a traditionally female role.

Voice and Choice

Many gay dads in this study described their emotions before they embarked on their journey to fatherhood. They said they felt a deep and abiding desire to parent, along with feelings of sadness that they, as men and as gays, could probably could not become dads. Although none recounted a specific incident of someone who forbade him to adopt, each man had experienced, from both the gay and the heterosexual communities, tacit messages that wanting to be a father meant that something was wrong with him. Nevertheless, they pursued their dream and in the process challenged and defied our cultural stereotypes about gays as safe and appropriate parents and about men as adequate in nurturing and caring for a child.

Overcoming other people's sexism and homophobia was not the only obstacle: Even before that, each man had to grapple with his own internalized sexism and homophobia. Many clinicians have noted that every gay person has an internal struggle to eradicate homophobia. Like nongay people, gay men and lesbians and bisexual people are raised in a social environment that abounds with negative messages and misinformation about being queer. Although these men had been out and well established in the gay community before they became dads, they still had to untangle their own lingering questions about whether they, as gay men, should become a father. And then, as men in a patriarchal society, they had to overcome their social conditioning to be focused on work and career advancement and buck the tide and become parents (a much less glamorous and unpaid position in our society). Additionally, because gay men constantly have to deal with the mainstream world's assaults on their manhood (i.e., tacit messages that gay men are not manly or not manly enough), they also had to deal with their feelings about crossing the gender line, doing something that, traditionally, was assigned to women. They had to ask themselves whether they felt that becoming a primary parent would make them less of a man. These issues were often subtle and hard to recognize and define but nevertheless were factors in their decision to parent.

After coming to terms with their own attitudes about manhood, gay manhood, and parenthood, the men then confronted the sexism of the child welfare system. Many revealed that, initially, even before they came out to anyone, their gender raised more eyebrows than any notions about their sexual orientation. In many states agency professionals were unwelcoming or uncooperative. As the men researched ways that they might become a parent, attended classes on adoption and foster care, went through training, completed reams of paperwork and the home study, opening their lives to scrutiny by complete strangers, they were reaffirming their commitment to become dads, whatever it took. Like the first women executives and the first women to become doctors, lawyers, and astronauts, these dads experienced both discomfort and a growing sense of entitlement to be whatever they wanted, not to be bound by society's gender-based limitations.

It may still be so today, but it was certainly true in the 1980s: Pursuing parenthood through foster care, adoption, and kinship care was not for the gay man who was even faintly ashamed of his gay identity. The men had to believe wholeheartedly that they would be appropriate parents, that they had good characters and inexhaustible love to give a child. They had to believe in themselves even when agencies and people in authority questioned their abilities and commitment. Again, we can see the parallels with feminist pioneers, who had to overcome skepticism, ridicule, and discrimination to be accepted in what was then a man's world.

As a well-educated, politically sophisticated, and financially stable group, the gay dads in the study were able to mobilize their resources and become articulate advocates for themselves. As activists who had already experienced discrimination and oppression in their lives, the men of color were especially experienced at rocking the boat in order to be heard. Of course, as men in a patriarchal society, they may have had a sense of entitlement, a sense that they had a right to be heard. It helped too that a collective voice was growing louder, with groups such as Center Kids in New

York and Pop Luck in Los Angeles, in advocating for the rights of gay dads.

Expanding Definitions of Parenthood

One of the most interesting themes that emerged in this study was how gay dads expanded society's definition of fatherhood by their primary involvement in their children's lives. In the context of the feminist revolution, which challenged gender-based roles in the family, these gay dads were able to imagine a new way to be fathers. Significantly, the men interviewed were able to parent their children in a dramatically different way than their own fathers had parented them. The men also remarked on how their definition of the role of father in the family was quite different from what they witnessed in the mostly heterosexual communities where they lived and raised their children.

Like other trailblazers, these gay dads were guided by their own inner compass, which directed them to be the fathers that their children needed and to resist the pull of the culture that told them that, as men, their focus should be outside the family. The images that our society has had of men parenting children include the divorced dad who sees the kids on the weekends and Thursday nights, the workaholic dad who just writes checks, and Mr. Mom, who pitches in with child care but still defers to the child's mother as the expert on what the child needs. The handful of heterosexual single fathers raising children alone for whatever reason are mostly invisible in our society, although those dads have always existed. In the 1980s gay fathers raising children without female coparents were also largely invisible. The gay dads in this study described how it felt to carve out a niche for their kind of fatherhood:

> As gay dads we are in a strange place. . . . In fact, I sometimes don't even think of myself as just a dad. . . . We are not like the traditional dads who work all day and then spend quality time with their children on the weekends

when they are off, but at the same time we are not like the moms, who usually have primary responsibility for their children, either. In some ways we are more than a dad, but we're not moms, either. I have to be a bit of a mom and a dad. I have to cook, clean, care for the child who is sick, read the bedtime story, do homework, and then play baseball, wrestle, and when necessary be the disciplinarian. I guess we really have had to define ourselves, just like gay people have had to do with everything that we have done in our lives.

Every father has to make sense of his own role in the family, the meaning of that role in his life, and his hopes and dreams of fatherhood. Gay dads go through this process too, working out ways to balance family and work and figure out their identity as a dad and as an individual. Each dad interviewed conveyed a certain mood and flow in his definition of fatherhood, and there were differences, as noted in their narratives, between the single dads, coupled dads, and separated dads.

Freer than most other kinds of dads from the dominant societal constraints associated with gender roles and parenting paradigms, the gay dads used their experiences in constructing adult identities as gay men when it was time to construct their own models of fatherhood. Both processes required the men to overcome social expectations, be true to their own values, and understand and accept themselves as worthy and good people.

Challenging Patriarchal Roles for Men

Traditionally, work defines men. The gay dads as a group rejected this model. Being the breadwinner was not how they wanted to define themselves as fathers. Although financially stable and comfortable in their lives, most of the gay dads in the study traded their intense focus on career self-definition through work to become primary caretakers of their children. This meant a different division of labor, which included work as a means to support the family, but they did not necessarily rely solely on work as a source of self-esteem. These dads expressed general satisfaction with their decision to focus more on parenting than on their career, but they were aware that they were breaking new ground. Some suggested that heterosexual fathers might have an easier time balancing work and fatherhood because the boundaries seemed clearer. In the narratives of coupled parents, one parent was more focused than the other on work as a means to support the family, while one parent was more focused on the home and child rearing. Single dads' narratives reflected a decreased interest in career advancement as their responsibilities in the family expanded.

Interestingly, the gay dads seldom defined their time and involvement with their children as work. Their narratives suggest that family work, as they see it, is something that brings them personal satisfaction. They were eloquent when describing caring for a child as a rich opportunity in which they were privileged to participate. Interestingly, several men noted how our culture undervalues this kind of family work, echoing generations of women who fought for respect and support in a male-dominated culture. Nevertheless, the gay dads reiterated that the most meaningful part of their lives was the privilege of parenting.

The narratives of these men suggest that they rejected the popular notion that men who do family work are special in some way or are heroes for breaking down cultural stereotypes. For them, the issue was not one of heroics or charging the gates of social convention. It was much simpler than that. Parenting was an urge of the heart, of the soul, not a social statement. Because of the context in which they were becoming dads, they became de facto activists, but the gay dads in the study emphasized that they did not become parents to prove a political point.

Finding Social Validation for Assuming a Traditionally Female Role

When the adults in their lives give little boys and little girls their first toys, the adults are establishing their expectations for the future. Gender socialization teaches boys and girls how to prepare for their adult lives. Even after decades of feminism, and even with the expectation that women will have careers and men will be more than just breadwinners, boys are encouraged to play with action figures that have destructive capabilities or superpowers. Girls receive dolls and learn how to dress and feed babies and sing them to sleep. Not all children engage in such stereotypical role-playing, but even if they do not, they seldom are introduced to the role-playing typical of the opposite gender. No one gives girls toy trucks and bulldozers; boys do not receive Barbie dolls. When men become fathers, they often feel awkward when changing diapers and preparing bottles. Over time, they learn how to handle the infant, talk to the toddler, comfort the child. In a family where there is a mother, a man can decide how much or how little he wants to participate. But gay dads do it all. While some of their heterosexual parenting counterparts (other moms at the playground, day care workers, and nursery school teachers) often welcomed them to the fold, each gay dad in the study experienced moments when he felt unwelcome and moments when he felt defensive, as if someone was challenging his ability to be a competent parent.

> As a gay dad, I'm not a mom, but sometimes I think I have more in common with moms than I do with straight dads. I mean, these straight dads that I know are essentially weekend dads; they don't parent with the same intensity that I do or that their wives do. In many ways, despite being a man, I am a dad, but I am like a mom too.
>
> I think what gets to me is when women who I don't know assume that because I am male that I am just like straight dads.

As these dads asserted their claim on core parts of the parenting repertoire, all described incidents when (often well-intentioned) women corrected or challenged their ability to care for their own child. All assumed that the criticism was based on a competitive feeling on the part of the women, that the women did not want to share what has traditionally been a female domain. Although those women may well have made similar comments to other women about their parenting styles, the gay dads experienced this criticism as fundamentally gender based, a blatant case of reverse sexism. Feminists have long suggested that we reexamine the subtle power structure of gender roles in the family. The presence of gay dads supports that notion as well. Yes, mothers play a unique and vital role in the rearing of children. And, yes, men, including gay men, who choose to be fathers play a unique and vital role in the rearing of children. The glass does not have to be half empty. The family does not have to define itself as a no-mommy family. As lesbian mothers, especially those raising boys, have learned, society looks askance at a single-parent family that does not provide children with same-sex role models. Gay fathers and lesbian mothers spend a lot of time explaining to the world that their family is happy and healthy despite having parents of only one gender. The idea that these families are inherently inadequate is not borne out by the research, which shows that children raised in lesbian-headed and gay-headed families are well adjusted, happy, and successful (Patterson 1995, 1996).

People who do not fit into what society has identified as the norm have always made the mainstream culture slightly uneasy. Society is clearly distressed, even in the twenty-first century, by men who choose to father children without the inherent benefits of a heterosexual union. "The knife of normalcy," notes Bloom (2002:113), "cuts sharp and crazy in our culture." The transformation has already begun, but it will take more time to change society's views of gay fatherhood so that these men receive the support and validation that they deserve.

Guidance and Direction for Child Welfare Professionals

I believe that the biggest roadblock to accepting and supporting gay fatherhood is our own attitudes and biases. Let's face it: Initiating a dialogue about gay men who are adopting, fostering, or parenting children through kinship relationships makes many people, including some child welfare professionals, uncomfortable. And this continues despite a sharp rise since the early 1990s in the number of gay men who are forming their own families through adoption, foster care, and kinship care. I would argue that we must consider the needs of the child first, no matter what our personal beliefs are about homosexuality or males as primary caregiver to a child.

The enactment of the historic Adoption and Safe Families Act (ASFA) of 1997 was the culmination of more than two decades of work to make it easier to move tens of thousands more children out of foster homes and into permanent families, including families headed by gay men. The new law provides unprecedented financial incentives to states to increase adoption and helps child welfare providers to speed children out of foster care and into permanent families by setting meaningful time limits for decisions, clarifying which family situations call for reasonable reunification efforts and which do not, and by making the safety of children the paramount concern in placement decisions (CWLA 1995b). Minimizing foster care drift and achieving permanency for children and youth (Maluccio, Fein, and Olmstead 1986; Pierce 1992; Pelton 1991) has been a principal focus of children, youth, and family services since 1980 and was reaffirmed in 1997 with enactment of ASFA.

Adoption historically was perceived as a preferential service for those couples, usually caucasian and infertile, who could afford to take a healthy same-race infant into their home. Today it is viewed in a much broader context. Contemporary adoption has made it possible for a broader range of children to be adopted: children of color; children with a range of disabilities, as well as those with medical and developmental issues; preschoolers and adolescents.

Similarly, policies have made it possible for a broader range of adults to adopt, including foster parents, families of color, single individuals (both male and female), older individuals, individuals with disabilities, and families across a broad economic range. At one time or another the adoption process excluded many of these groups. In fact, the inclusion of some of these groups caused great controversy at first. In moving toward inclusiveness, many professionals voiced concern about lowering the standard of adoption and damaging the field. While the field of children, youth, and families services has broadened its vision of adoption, some in the field have cautioned that professionals must always focus on finding families for children, not on finding children for families.

No accurate statistics exist on the number of gay people in the United States, but Kinsey estimated that as much as 10 percent of the population (twenty-five million individuals) identify as being nonheterosexual. Does it really make sense to exclude twenty-five million potential adoptive parents solely on the basis of sexual orientation? Study after study has found that pedophiles overwhelmingly are heterosexuals, even those who commit same-sex abuse. Research also consistently shows that children of lesbian and gay parents are happy and successful in school and in the world. Are we worried that these kids might grow up to be gay? Just look at the parents of gay people, nearly all of whom were raised by heterosexuals. Clearly, sexual orientation is not something a parent can influence. Thus the only real problem is our own prejudice. It is time to push past that and consider the children. They need loving families. We cannot continue to discriminate against gay people who would be loving adoptive parents. In fact, the children need them.

Although some child welfare agencies are struggling to develop policies regarding gay and lesbian adoption, many agencies appear to believe "the less said the better" (Sullivan 1995:3). Some of this "don't ask, don't tell" attitude undoubtedly stems in part from the fear of being stigmatized as "the gay adoption agency." In the absence of written policies, staff members often develop their own policies, based on their personal beliefs. The lack of written policies is a strategy in and of itself, and many child welfare agency executives and boards have permitted this situation to exist so that they can dodge controversy. But this does not serve the children who are waiting for homes. When individuals are guided by their own personal beliefs rather than clearly written policies, agencies run the risk of exercising personal, cultural, and religious bias when deciding who may parent. What if the agency worker believes that Christians should not be allowed to adopt? Or single women? Or African Americans? Child welfare agencies that take this pusillanimous approach and don't wrestle with their biases also do the community a disservice. How can we resolve the issue as neighbors, voters, and taxpayers? Policies that address the needs of children and families need to be written and clearly communicated to all interested groups.

Policy Development Versus Prejudice

The creation of gay-headed adoptive, foster, and kinship care families is an intensely emotional and divisive topic. We often polarize those who are in favor of gay rights and those who are antigay. I would like us to reconsider the terms of this debate. Who is interested in what is best for children? The challenge to child welfare professionals is not to please everyone, not to pander to politics, but to develop a rational position that is based on professional values, available research, and experience. Child welfare agencies that wish to develop policies regarding adoption and foster parenting by gay men need to reflect on a number of questions: How should a child welfare organization respond to gay men who want to adopt or foster children? If a child welfare agency accepts a gay applicant, what will be the response of its board, its community constituents, and its funding sources? How should a child welfare organization respond to media attention or attacks from the radical right? Do gay men have the "right" to adopt? Is it fair for a child to be placed in a gay adoptive or foster home? If a child welfare agency does not accept a gay applicant, is there potential for legal liability? Can an agency be sued for failing to accept or for accepting a gay applicant? How much do professionals in a particular child welfare organization know about gay men as potential adoptive or foster parents?

Policy Development

Sound policy is developed based on information from external sources and from child welfare practice wisdom. Unfortunately, most policy is developed with less-than-complete information and sometimes without a thoughtful process of discernment. All policies undoubtedly have political consequences (DiNitto 1995; Taylor 1994), but policies are not set in stone. Flexibility is required to accommodate changing environmental conditions and situations, which in turn require policy modification or change. Since the 1980s the child welfare community has responded in an adaptive way in several key areas: culturally diverse communities, substance-abusing populations, and those affected by HIV/AIDS.

Agency leaders have resources to help them figure out their policies and get accurate information. The gay parenting community has several on-line resources and a growing professional literature (*Kids' Talk* 1999; Family Tree 1998), and some professionals have years of wisdom and insights from working with gay and lesbian parents. Additionally, the National Adoption Information Clearinghouse (2000); the Northwest Adoption Exchange (Nelson 1997); and the Adoption Resource Exchange for Single Parents (A. Beers 1977; Solot 1998) have developed and disseminated important information for gay adoptive parents. Such information can provide an accurate impression of the range of family options that exist in the gay community and can highlight their potential as adoptive resources for children awaiting foster or adoptive homes.

I have adapted from Sullivan's work (1995:5–8) the following considerations for professionals who are developing policy, and I offer them here as guidelines for developing a more affirming approach to working with gay men who are interested in becoming parents:

1. The primary client is the child in need of a permanent family All families are potential resources for the child. The issue is not whether gay men have the right to create families. No person has the right to adopt or to be a foster parent; these are privileges afforded to those individuals and couples who meet a standard. All individuals should be given equal consideration as potential adoptive parents.

2. All permanency considerations should focus on the best interests of the child. Child welfare professionals should ask, "What is the best permanency resource for this child at this time?"

3. No single factor, including sexual orientation, should be the determining factor in assessing suitability for adoption, foster, or kinship care parenting.

4. The capacity to nurture a child and a parent's sexual orientation are separate issues. These must not be confused in decision making.

5. Gay applicants should be assessed with the same criteria as all other prospective parents. Although gay adoptive, foster, or kinship care parents may present some unique situations for a practitioner to assess, they should not have to pass extraordinary means tests to prove their worthiness as parents. Child welfare professionals should make use of an excellent publication made available by the Adoption Resource Exchange for Single Parents, *Guidelines for Adoption Workers: Writing Lesbian, Gay, Bisexual, and Transgender Homestudies for Special Needs Adoptions* (Solot 1998). In making such an assessment, those working to certify gay parents should ask themselves, "What are their individual strengths or weaknesses, and what is their capacity to nurture a child or children who were not born to them?"

6. Each permanency decision should be based on the strengths and needs of the child and the perceived ability of the prospective parent to meet those needs and develop those strengths.

Given the responsibilities of child welfare agencies to the children they are placing, child welfare professionals should thoughtfully identify the array of issues involved in a family where a gay parent or parents raise a child. Obviously, these families have more similarities to those with nongay parents than differences. Child welfare agencies should examine all families for emotional maturity, flexibility, and openness. If two partners are applying to be adoptive parents, professionals should be able to evaluate the commitment that they have toward one another and the stability of the relationship; if the potential adoptive parent is single, professionals will need to carefully examine the individual's existing support networks. Furthermore, professionals will also be called upon to evaluate the parent's experience with children and the ability to distinguish a child's need from the parent's.

Some aspects of foster parenting or adoption by gay people are different from fostering or adoption by heterosexuals. Child welfare organizations should evaluate the following issues:

- Most states legally recognize only one same-gender partner as a parent. Although this is changing in some states (i.e., New Jersey), child welfare professionals should be aware of the consequences for the child of having a legal and nonlegal parent and must also assist potential adoptive parents in negotiating a careful discussion of this issue.
- How willing are the parents to be open about their sexual orientation within their community? Having a child who attends school, makes use of health care services, and attends other child-oriented recreational events may cause parents to make decisions according to their own comfort level.
- How willing are the parents to deal with and openly address the multiple levels of "differentness" that they and their child will experience? All adopted children face issues related to their sense of differentness about being adopted, but some types of differentness are easier to deal with than other types.
- As with all permanency decisions, children and youth should be involved in the decision-making process whenever possible. For example, in placing a twelve-year-old with a gay couple, it would be important to determine what the child knows about gay people and gauge his or her understanding of the benefits and challenges evident in placement with a specific family.
- Although critics often point to the supposed deficits of gay men, they are incredibly resilient individuals and as such bring a great many strengths to a family. Gay men know firsthand how important it is to allow children to develop naturally, without preconceived notions about what a child should be. Creating a family required all gay men to examine their motives. Determined to become parents through adoption, foster care, or relative care, and to provide healthy and nurturing environments for their children, these gay dads enjoyed parenting and worked hard at it. In general,

these fathers were strong, stable individuals who have made a commitment to children. They believe that creating a family through adoption, foster care, or relative care is a rewarding and enriching experience. Because of this strong commitment they promote significant positive outcomes in the lives of their children. Child welfare professionals should be aware of the multiple strengths of a gay-headed family and view these strengths as a viable resource for children in need of permanent and loving homes.

Consequences of Inaction

Child welfare systems that seek to avoid the issue of parenting by gay-headed families are likely to face the following consequences.

A continuation in the trend toward private independent adoption rather than agency adoption, because prospective parents who are gay will find other means to fulfill their desires to parent.

An increased likelihood of legal action against agencies, whether through individual suits brought by parents or class actions brought on their behalf. Many states constitutionally or statutorily prohibit discrimination on the basis of sexual orientation. Increasingly, gay men are turning to litigation in response to discrimination. All too often such actions result in a court's making the decisions that the state's professionals should but were unable to make.

The continued expenditure of public funds to maintain children in out-of-home care for longer periods than would be necessary if agencies considered all families as resources.

The likelihood that a number of children would not be placed in a family at all (children born HIV positive were an example of this), when they could have been adopted by a gay-headed family.

Not all gay men should be parents, but the same can be said of nongay people. Many gay men, as evidenced by the narratives discussed herein and the experience of thousands of others, can be wonderful, caring, and loving parents for children who need a permanent home and a loving family. They can also make mistakes, get frustrated, feel isolated and alone—in short, they are the same as any other parent. The question is not whether gay men will be approved as adoptive, foster, or kinship care parents but how publicly this will be done and whether these families will be offered the same opportunities as others to adopt. Sidestepping the issue of adoption, foster, and kinship care parenting by gay men does not protect children. It actually runs counter to the law and to the Adoption and Safe Families Act because it prevents competent and caring adults from providing permanent families for children in need. It prevents some children from being part of a loving family, which all children deserve. Child welfare systems are responsible for ensuring a timely and appropriate permanent living arrangement for every child. In meeting this responsibility, child welfare agencies must explore all potential resources for every single child awaiting placement in a family. The time has come to openly include, and support, gay men who have the desire to parent and a longing to share their lives with a child who needs a family. Who would deny this love and nurturing to a child?

Appendix

Field Experience
in Retrospect

I began this study in 1999 as part of unfunded research that I had been interested in pursuing. Largely because of my twenty-eight years of professional experience in child welfare systems in New York and nationally, and also because I am an openly gay man and a parent, I always felt comfortable when working with openly gay men who had decided to become parents.

Given that almost no research exists about gay men who have chosen to become fathers, and given the many parallels between grounded theory research and direct practice, using a grounded theory approach seemed warranted. Because the methods of this approach are steeped in the natural world, many social work practitioners use it (Gilgun 1994:115). "Real world problems," notes Schon, "do not come well-formed. Instead, they tend to present themselves as problematic situations, messy and indeterminate" (1995:34). The process of doing grounded theory research, with all its ambiguity and its messiness, seemed natural to me as a practitioner.

Grounded Theory

The roots of the grounded theory movement lie in the work of two sociologists at the University of California, Barney Glaser and Anselm Strauss, who studied the experiences of hospital personnel with dying patients (Glaser and Strauss 1965). They more thoroughly articulated their approach in a subsequent 1967 text, expanded upon and refined it in other work (Glaser 1978, 1992; Strauss 1987; Strauss and Corbin 1990), and saw others use it (Charmaz 1990; Gerson 1991; Gilgun 1994; Mizrahi and Abramson 1994) in promoting a research process for promoting adequate sociological theory.

The original work of Glaser and Strauss (1967) sought to promote a research process for developing sociological theory. They believed that adequate theory could emerge only from intensive involvement with the phenomenon under study. "Grounded theory" is described as a method by which theory is induced through empirical observation; this model provided the theoretical basis for my study.

Doing Grounded Theory Research

In attempting to take a fresh look at and work toward discovering the multiple experiences of gay men who had chosen to become fathers, I used the methodology of grounded theory to develop theories; this process helped me find ways to define concepts, relationships among those concepts, and processes (Gilgun 1994:116).

While I was researching the multiple experiences of these gay fathers, I was determined to remain open to the data and my own biases and to approach the project without hypothesis or preconceived notions about what I would find. As the research proceeded, I began to define concepts, to see relationships among concepts, and to discern patterns. I attempted to continually compare my emerging empirical findings with new data. I continually modified my findings to fit the data, a process that caused me to continually define and redefine concepts and relationships among concepts. Such data collection and data analysis involve a series of comparisons. As such, the research effort is a process of discovery and reformulation, what Glaser and Strauss term "constant comparative method," a phrase that connotes the continual comparisons done within and across cases. Grounded theory requires a line-by-line analysis and constant comparison of data while searching for themes and/or categories. This method entails further research into the meaning of the developing categories by further sampling from appropriate participants or other data sources. Then I wove together the codes and categories to tell a story about gay men who choose to be fathers. The constant comparisons that this method requires yielded a theory that speaks to the experiences of gay men who choose to be fathers.

Gilgun notes that "the concepts and the hypotheses developed through these processes are inextricably linked to the empirical world, hence the name grounded theory" (1994:116). These links are presented clearly in the findings, along with the more abstract concepts and hypotheses and the concrete data that support them.

Data Collection Methods

I used open-ended semistructured interviews and participant observation to collect data. Open-ended interviews were the primary means, as they allowed respondents to describe what was meaningful and salient without being pigeonholed. Because I used open-ended interviews, my results emphasize the multiple experiences and points of view of the informants.

Involvement with Informants

Observing and interviewing the twenty subjects for this study brought me into the social world of my informants. This study took place in the natural settings where these dads lived their lives, usually in their homes or in a restaurant over multiple cups of coffee. To explore the many experiences and to examine the strategies used by gay dads to create their families, I conducted and taped in-depth interviews with the men as well as one important informant, who was not a dad but had significant information to share about fathers and about gay parenting in general.

I used one interview protocol (which I will make available upon request). In an effort to assess the clarity of the questions and their ability to evoke responses that describe the experience of the gay dads, I tested the protocol with three dads I knew. I asked the interviewees for their reactions to the questions and the order which I asked them, as well as suggestions for improvement and for any other questions that they believed might help me get at the material I was seeking. I also used these test interviews to assess the value of taping. Because this research was exploratory and the emphasis was on using descriptive material for conceptual development, I did not use the explicit content of these interviews in the final report.

Informants

The interview guide focused on eight major areas of inquiry for these dads, namely, their descriptions of their first awareness of the desire to become a father; their relationship with their family of origin; their relationship with the gay community; descriptions of their initial parenting experiences; how they went about building their family; the response of the community; and recommendations for changes in the child welfare system to facilitate adoptions, foster care, and kinship care for gay men who want to become parents. I identified preliminary questions for each area and used probes to follow up with additional questions. The questions were designed to elicit examples, critical incidents, and descriptive details and to capture the positive and negative experiences of pursuing and becoming fathers. I told the men that the focus of the interviews would be their reflections on their first awareness of the desire to parent, their subsequent experiences in becoming a parent, and their own attitudes about gay men who choose to become fathers. I also told them that I wanted to know their ideas about how to reform the child welfare system to make it more positively responsive to gay men who wish to pursue parenting through foster care, adoption, or kinship care.

In New York, where I began the study, I placed notices at the Lesbian and Gay Community Services Center and left specially prepared flyers at both mainstream child welfare agencies and at support agencies that gay parents are known to use. These announcements included a phone number that the men were to use to arrange for an appointment for an interview. In Los Angeles, where I had extensive contacts with professional colleagues, I visited the members of the Pop Luck group and provided those dads who were interested with contact information to set up an interview. To supplement these data collection approaches, I sought interviews from dads recommended by their peers and acquaintances.

Professional Informants

I interviewed only one professional staff person for this study, Terry Boggis, and I used an interview guide that followed a format similar to the one I used for the fathers. In this case the interview focused on issues of service delivery, namely, general knowledge of and ability to identify the population; knowledge of resources; knowledge of the needs of the population; general impressions about the gay dads from various child welfare professionals; racial, cultural, or religious issues with respect to this population; issues regarding training; and recommendations for changes.

I used the interview with Boggis to corroborate the dads' experiences. Data from this interview are woven into the fabric of the book. I contacted Boggis by telephone to schedule an interview date and time that was convenient for the person. The interview took place in this professional's office.

I guaranteed all informants anonymity and total confidentiality, pledges that were printed on the consent form that they received and were asked to sign at the time of the face-to-face interview. The time allotted to each person varied considerably, depending on his schedule, but the average interview lasted two hours.

Data Analysis

In qualitative research approaches the data are almost always words, here in the form of fieldnotes, audiotapes, and documents. Managing the data from twenty-one transcribed interviews was challenging and was done with content analysis. I obtained, recorded, entered into the computer, and coded all interview data using a computer software program (Seidel, Kjolseth, and Seymour 1988) that helped me manage the information.

Grounded theory begins with basic descriptions and moves to conceptual ordering by organizing the data into categories. The process uses description to elucidate the categories. The final step is theorizing, formulating the data into logical, systematic, and explanatory schemes (Strauss and Corbin 1998:21).

This process has enabled me to code data with an open coding scheme and thus create an analytic process for identifying key concepts and their properties and discerning their dimensions in the data (Strauss and Corbin 1998:101). This coding scheme allowed me to label concepts that represent discrete happenings and to describe other instances of the phenomenon. The descriptive narratives about the central phenomenon of the study, the experiences of gay men choosing to be fathers, permitted me to classify and identify themes in categories, which led me to develop my own conceptualization of the story. The attributes and characteristics that pertain to the themes and categories then lead to the development of theoretical constructs to explain the phenomenon of gay men choosing to become fathers. All grounded theory studies use a data-coding scheme to categorize data rather than to quantify it. Using a system of open coding permitted me to explicate the stories of these gay men, identifying themes and relationships and then validating those relationships against the data by filling in categories with other data as necessary.

Grounded theory methods are oriented toward exploration, discovery, and inductive reasoning. In my analysis of the data from the narratives of these twenty men, I began with specific observations and built toward general patterns, categories, and dimensions of analysis that emerged from the open-ended interviews and observations. This strategy allowed important analytic dimensions to emerge from patterns found in the cases studied without predetermining what the important dimensions would be.

The themes of gay men choosing to be fathers emerged from analysis of the data in two ways: as indigenous topologies and as analyst-generated topologies. The first, categories developed and articulated by the men studied, organized the presentation of particular subsidiary categories around the central story line. The second category developed as I became aware of categories or story lines for which the informants did not have labels or terms; for these I have developed terms to describe these inductively generated categories.

Trusting that themes and patterns would emerge from the collection of data through the semistructured interviews, I searched for analogues to understand them, when necessary using the professional literature in the areas of fatherhood, parenting, and adoption; and I tried to be conscious of the respondents' use of metaphor to describe phenomena and searched for similarities in different patterns and concepts.

The findings are focused on understanding individual situations and testing to see whether findings in one or multiple situations can illuminate and be relevant in validating these relationships against other situations. This process of testing to determine whether previous findings are relevant to a new situation is called pattern matching, or testing for goodness of fit.

Analysis with grounded theory data that yields thick description (Geertz 1973) is a time-consuming, multidimensional, and labor-intensive process that required me to live for as long as possible with the complexities and ambiguities of the stories that informants presented to me, as I tried to come to terms with them and ultimately to present them to the reader in a form that clarifies and deepens them (Miles and Huberman 1984:251). This was also a process of resisting the temptation for premature closure and developing an ability to live with the complexity. I relied on theoretical sensitivity, which indicates an awareness of the subtleties of meaning of the data. In an attempt to remain bias free, and to produce a valid and reliable theory, I frequently had to challenge myself to periodically step back from the data to remain objective, to maintain an attitude of skepticism, and to follow the research procedures of good science. Throughout this study I asked colleagues grounded in practice and theory to help me reflect on the data, realizing that someone who was not immersed in it could sometimes see and/or validate dimensions that I could not see. I also used this procedure to ensure the reliability of the data (Drisko 1997) and as a check against my own inherent bias.

Ultimately, because qualitative analysis to uncover themes, patterns, and categories is a creative process, I had to make carefully considered judgments about what were truly significant and meaningful data in the explication of the story. Without statistical tests to inform me when a pattern that I observed was significant, I had to rely on my own intelligence, experience, and judgment. As I was doing this, I was aware of difference, of particularity, of that which was contradictory, and of that which was paradoxical. As a result, I realized that what I was finding may have been quantitatively insignificant, but the finding itself may have led me to question a more conventional interpretation and expand my understanding (Opie 1992). I was also aware throughout this process that the experiences of these twenty dads could not be broadly generalized to all gay fathers, because these informants could speak only about their own experiences. Throughout these investigations I kept in mind these hazards and criteria for assessing qualitative data analysis, as elaborated upon elsewhere by others (Altheide and Johnson 1994; Drisko 1997; Guba and Lincoln 1981; Reid 1994), and I hope my deliberate effort has minimized the risks.

The stories in this book and their interpretations remark on the experiences of gay men who choose to be fathers through adoption, foster care, and kinship care outside the boundaries of a heterosexual union. This study depicts, in twenty versions, both the incongruity of and the resemblance to the culture's versions of gay men as fathers and the lived experiences of gay men as fathers. The decision of these men to share their lives accords us rich opportunities to be open to the unfolding of local knowledge on which direct practice can be, and indeed should be, built. In exploring such inclinations, one must proceed with care. In abandoning the role of "expert" and instead entering into a collaborative search for meaning with subjects, I wished to create openness to local knowledge, to listen to these men's voices, to their narratives, and to their constructions of reality. In doing so, I wished to present a study that is grounded in the subjects' experience and that can speak in the voices of men who had been told for most of their lives that they were never to be close to children. This strategy presents a very different scenario than that of the large-scale epidemiological studies. This study examines the particular, pays attention to difference, and, most vital, allows multiple voices to emerge to tell their own story. As such, the questions that I asked and the interpretations of the data that I offer in this book developed in collaboration with the gay dads, who are, after all, the experts.

This study was guided theoretically throughout by the work of Glaser and Strauss (1967). I also kept in mind the historian Barbara Tuchman's advice to submit oneself to the material instead of trying to impose oneself on the material (1979:37). This provided additional direction for this study, granting me permission to step aside and allow the data to ultimately speak to and supply the answers. In modeling my own work after the work of these scholars, I too hope to permit these fathers to tell their own story in their own words and hope in the process that their narratives help to redefine contemporary notions about fatherhood.

The stories and narratives of gay fathers described here replace the myths with first-person reflections, the necessary components for the development of local knowledge (Geertz 1983; Hartman 1990, 1992, 1994). Another major gift that these gay dads offer is a first-person account of what it is like to want to parent and nurture a child while being invisible and invalidated by a society that presumes that all parents are heterosexual and that primary parenting is women's work. Disempowerment strategies used by dominant groups, as well as the technological pollution that endangers the health and well-being of individuals, imposed enormous adaptive tasks on the men interviewed. The effects of adapting to an environment that constantly challenges your desires and abilities to be a parent can be far-reaching and devastating to one's psychological state, but the men in this study were resilient and strong parents, showing little evidence of the effects of the disempowerment and social pollution that are expressions of destructive relationships between the person and environments.

Gay Men Choosing Parenthood is one of the first studies to examine the experiences of gay men who have chosen to parent, and I hope that it will be the first step in assisting the field of children, youth, and family services in its further exploration and examination of this important issue.

References

Altheide, D. and J. Johnson. 1994. Criteria for assessing the interpretive validity in qualitative research. In N. Denzin and Y. Lincoln, eds., *Handbook of qualitative research*, pp. 485–99. Thousand Oaks, Calif.: Sage.

American Psychological Association. 1995. *Lesbian and gay parenting: Resource for psychologists*. Washington, D.C.: APA.

Arizona law gives gay foster parents edge. 1997. *Phoenix Times*, November 13, p. A3.

Arnold, T. 1997. Protect foster kids from gay discrimination. *Edmonton (Canada) Journal*, July 16, p. 31

Baker, P. 1997. Clinton signs law to speed adoption process for children in foster care. *Washington Post*, November 20, p. A17.

Baldauf, S. 1997. How Texas wrestles with gay adoptions. *Christian Science Monitor*, December 3, p. 3.

Barbell, K. and M. Freundlich. 2001. *Foster care today*. Washington, D.C.: Casey Family Programs.

Barnett, R. C. and G. K. Baruch. 1988. Correlates of father's participation in family work. In P. Bronstein and C. P. Cowen, eds., *Fatherhood today*, pp. 76–78. New York: John Wiley.

Barret, B. and B. E. Robinson. 2000. *Gay fathers*. 2d ed. Lexington, Mass.: Lexington Books.

Baruch, G. K. and R. C. Barnett. 1983. *Correlates of father's participation in family work: A technical report*. Wellesley, Mass.: Wellesley College Center for Research on Women.

Beers, A. (1977). *The tale of two families: Gay men and lesbians building loving families*. Springfield, Va.: Adoption Resource Exchange for Single Parents.

Bell, A. P. and M. S. Weinberg. 1978. *Homosexualities: A study of diversity among men and women*. New York: Simon and Schuster.

Benkov, L. 1994. *Reinventing the family: The emerging story of lesbian and gay parents*. New York: Crown.

Bernfeld, R. 1995. A brief guide regarding donor and co-parenting agreements. In M. E. Elovitz and C. Schneider, eds., *Legal issues facing the nontraditional family — 1995*, pp. 135–69. New York: Practicing Law Institute.

Bigner, J. 1996. Working with gay fathers. In J. Laird and R.-J. Green, eds., *Lesbians and gays in couples and families: A handbook for therapists*, pp. 370–403. San Francisco: Jossey-Bass.

Bigner, J. J. and R. W. Bozett. 1989. Parenting by gay fathers. *Marriage and Family Review* 15(3–4): 155–75.

Bigner, J. J. and R. R. Jacobsen. 1989a. Parenting behaviors of homosexual and heterosexual fathers. *Journal of Homosexuality* 18(1–2): 173–86.

————. 1989b. The value of children for gay versus nongay fathers. *Journal of Homosexuality* 18(1–2): 163–72.

Biller, H. B. and J. L. Kimpton. 1997. The father and the school-aged child. In M. E. Lamb, ed., *The role of the father in child development*, pp. 143–61. New York: John Wiley.

Blankenhorn, D. 1995. *Fatherless America*. New York: Basic Books.

Blau, E. 1993. *Stories of adoption*. Portland, Ore.: New Sage Press.

Bloom, A. 2002. *Normal*. New York: Random House.

Bozett, F. W. 1987. *Gay and lesbian parents*. New York: Praeger.

————. 1989. *Homosexuality and the family*. New York: Harrington Park Press.

Brazelton, T. B. 1992. *Touchpoints: Your child's emotional and behavioral development*. Reading, Mass.: Perseus.

Brodzinsky, D. M. and M. D. Schechter, eds. 1990. *The psychology of adoption*. New York: Oxford.

Brodzinsky, D. M., M. D. Schechter, and R. Marantz. 1993. *Being adopted: The lifelong search for self*. New York: Anchor.

Bryant, A. S. and R. Demian. 1994. Relationship characteristics of American gay and lesbian couples: Findings from a national survey. In L. A. Kurdek, ed., *Social services for gay and lesbian couples*, pp. 101–17. New York: Haworth.

Charmaz, K. 1990. Discovering chronic illness: Using grounded theory. *Social Science and Medicine* 30(11): 1161–72.

Children's Bureau. 2000. Promising practices: States streamline foster and adoptive home approval process. *Children's Bureau Express* 1, no. 7 (November): 1–4.

Children's Bureau. 2003. *AFCARS data tables.* www.acf.dhhs.gov/programs/cb/publications/afcars/report8.htm (March 31, 2003).

Colberg, M. 1996. With open arms: The emotional journey of lesbian and gay adoption. *In the Family* 2, no. 1 (fall): 6–11.

————. 2001. LGBT people can be particularly good parents of adoptees. *In the Family* 7, no. 2 (summer): 7, 26.

Court refuses challenge to gay foster placements. 1997. *Boston Globe,* October 7, p. 43.

Cowan, C. P. and P. A. Cowan. 1988. Who does what when partners become parents? Implications for men, women, and marriage. *Marriage and Family Review* 13:105–32.

————. 1992. *When partners become parents: The big life change for couples.* New York: Basic Books.

Cowan, P. A., C. P. Cowan, and P. K. Kerig. 1993. Mothers, fathers, sons, and daughters: Gender differences in family formation and parenting style. In P. A. Cowan, D. Field et al., eds., *Family, self, and society: Toward a new agenda for family research,* pp. 165–95. Hillsdale, N.J.: Erlbaum.

Cowan, P. A. et al. 1985. Transitions to parenthood: His, hers, and theirs. *Journal of Family Issues* 6:451–81.

Cramer, D. 1986. Gay parents and their children: A review of research and practical implications. *Journal of Counseling and Development* 64:501–7.

Crumbley, J. 1999. *Transracial adoption and foster care.* Washington, D.C.: CWLA Press.

Crumbley, J. and R. Little. 1997. *Relatives raising children: An overview of kinship care.* Washington, D.C.: CWLA Press.

Cummings, E. M. and A. W. O'Reilly. 1997. Fathers in family context: Effects of marital quality on child adjustment. In M. E. Lamb, ed., *The role of the father in child development,* pp. 49–65. New York: John Wiley.

CWLA (Child Welfare League of America). 1988. *Standards for adoption.* Washington, D.C.: Child Welfare League of America.

————. 1995. *Standards of excellence for family foster care.* Washington, D.C.: Child Welfare League of America.

————. 2000. *Standards of excellence for kinship care.* Washington, D.C.: Child Welfare League of America.

Dienhart, A. 1998. *Reshaping fatherhood: The social construction of shared parenting.* Thousand Oaks, Calif.: Sage.

DiNitto, D. M. 1995. *Social welfare politics and public policy.* 4th ed. Engelwood Cliffs, N.J.: Prentice Hall.

Dougherty, S. 2001. *Toolbox no. 2: Expanding the role of foster parents in achieving permanency.* Washington, D.C.: Child Welfare League of America.

Drisko, J. W. 1997. Strengthening qualitative studies and reports: Standards to promote academic integrity. *Journal of Social Work Education* 33(1): 185–97.

Dunlap, D. W. 1996. Homosexual parent raising children: Support for pro and con. *New York Times,* January 7, p. L15.

Dunn, J. 1999. *From one child to two.* New York: Random House.

Dunne, E. J. 1991. Helping gay fathers come out to their children. *Journal of Homosexuality* 14(1–2): 213–22.

Elovitz, M. E. 1995. Adoption by lesbian and gay people: The use and misuse of social science research. In M. E. Elovitz and C. Schneider, eds., *Legal issues facing the nontraditional family—1995,* pp. 171–91. New York: Practicing Law Institute.

Family Tree. 1998. *The family tree.* San Diego: Family Pride Coalition.

Fanshel, D. 1982. *On the road to permanency: An expanded data base for children in foster care.* New York: Child Welfare League of America.

Fanshel, D. and E. Shinn. 1978. *Children in foster care: A longitudinal investigation.* New York: Columbia University Press.

Feigelman, W. and A. S. Silverman. 1983. *Chosen children: New patterns of adoptive relationships.* New York: Praeger.

Ferrero, E., J. Freker, and T. Foster. 2002. *Too high a price: The case against restricting gay parenting.* New York: ACLU: Lesbian and Gay Rights Project.

Festinger, T. 1983. *No one ever asked us: A post script to foster care.* New York: Columbia University Press.

Florida judge upholds state gay adoption ban. 1997. *Miami Herald,* July 29, p. 33.

Foster parent adoption: What professionals should know. 2000. *National Adoption Information Clearinghouse.* December 21.

Freiberg, P. 1999 Gay adoption rights under attack. *New York Blade,* January 22, pp. 1, 7.

Frommer, M. S. 1996. The right fit: A gay man's quest for fatherhood. *In the Family* 2, no.1 (fall): 12–16, 26.

Gay Rights Project. 1999. *American Civil Liberties Union.* www.aclu.org (November 20, 2002).

Geertz, C. 1973. *The interpretation of culture*. New York: Basic Books.
———. 1983. *Local knowledge: Further essays in interpretive Anthropology*. New York: Basic Books.
Georgia ban on gay adoption in committee. 1998. *Atlanta Times*, March 10, p. 2.
Gerson, E. M. 1991. Supplementing grounded theory. In D. R. Maines, ed., *Social organization and social process: Essays in honor of Anselm Strauss*, pp. 285–301. New York: Aldine de Gruyter.
Gilgun, J. 1994. Hand into glove: The grounded theory approach and social work practice research. In E. Sherman and W. Reid, eds., *Qualitative research in social work*, pp. 115–25. New York: Columbia University Press.
Glaser, B. G. 1978. *Theoretical sensitivity*. Mill Valley, Calif.: Sociological Press.
———. 1992. *Basics of grounded theory analysis*. Mill Valley, Calif.: Sociological Press.
Glaser, B. G. and A. L. Strauss. 1965. *Awareness of dying*. Hawthorne, N.Y.: Aldine.
———. 1967. *The discovery of grounded theory: Strategies for qualitative research*. Chicago: Aldine.
Goldman, J. D. G. and R. J. Goldman. 1983. Children's perceptions of parents and their roles: A cross-national study in Australia, England, North America, and Sweden. *Sex Roles* 9:791–812.
Golombok, S., A. Spencer, and M. Rutter. 1983. Children in lesbian and single-parent households: Psychosexual and psychiatric appraisal. *Journal of Child Psychology and Psychiatry* 24:551–72.
Gordon, T. 2000. *Parent effectiveness training: The proven program for raising responsible children*. New York: Three Rivers Press.
Green, A. A. 1999. Board votes to ban gays as providers of foster care. *Arkansas Democratic Gazette*, January 7, pp. 1, 5A.
Green, G. D. and F. W. Bozett. 1991. Lesbian mothers and gay fathers. In J. C. Gonsiorek and J. C. Weinrich, eds., *Homosexuality: Research implications for public policy*, pp. 197–214. Thousand Oaks, Calif.: Sage.
Green, J. 1999. *The velveteen father: An unexpected journey to parenthood*. New York: Villard.
Griswold, R. L. 1993. *Fatherhood in America*. New York: Basic Books.
Grossman, F. R., W. S. Pollack, and E. Golding. 1988. Fathers and children: Predicting the quality and quantity of fathering. *Developmental Psychology* 24:82–91.
Groth, A. N. 1978. Patterns of sexual assault against children and adolescents. In A. W. Burgess, A. N. Groth, L. L. Holmstrom,

and S. M. Sgroi, eds., *Sexual assault of children and adolescents,*
pp. 3–24. Lexington, Mass.: Lexington Books.

Groth, A. N. and H. J. Birnbaum. 1978. Adult sexual orientation and
attraction to underage persons. *Archives of Sexual Behavior* 7(3):
175–181.

Guba, E. and Y. Lincoln. 1981. *Effective evaluation.* San Francisco:
Jossey-Bass.

Hamer, J. 2001. *What it means to be daddy: Fatherhood for black men
living away from their children.* New York: Columbia University
Press.

Hartman, A. 1990. Many ways of knowing. Editorial. *Social Work*
35(1): 3–4.

———. 1992. In search of subjugated knowledge. Editorial. *Social
Work* 37(6): 483–84.

———. 1994. Setting the theme: Many ways of knowing. In
E. Sherman and W. Reid, eds., *Qualitative research in social work,*
pp. 459–63. New York: Columbia University Press.

———. 1996. Social policy as a context for lesbian and gay families:
The political is personal. In J. Laird and R.-J. Green, eds.,
Lesbians and gays in couples and families: A handbook for therapists,
pp. 69–85. San Francisco: Jossey-Bass.

Hartman, A. and J. Laird. 1998. Moral and ethical issues in working
with lesbians and gay men. *Families in society* 31:263–76.

Hennie, M. A. 1999. Historic second term may set agenda for
presidential bid: Texas Gov. Bush joined the bandwagon
opposing gay/lesbian adoption and parenting. *Impact,* January
29, p. 1.

Herek, G. M. 1991. Stigma, prejudice, and violence against lesbians
and gay men. In J. C. Gonsiorek and J. D. Weinrich, eds.,
Homosexuality: Research implications for public policy, pp. 60–80.
Newbury Park, Calif.: Sage.

Hetherington, E. M. and L. A. Stanley-Hagan. 1997. The effects of
divorce on fathers and their children. In M. E. Lamb, ed., *The
role of the father in child development,* pp. 191–211. New York:
John Wiley.

Hochschild, A. R. 1995. Understanding the future of fatherhood:
The daddy hierarchy and beyond. In M. C. P. van Dongen,
G. A. B. Frinking, and M. J. G. Jacobs, eds., *Changing father-
hood: An interdisciplinary perspective,* pp. 219–30. Amsterdam:
Thesis.

Horn, W. F. and T. Sylvester. 2002. *Father facts.* 4th ed. Lancaster, Pa.:
National Fatherhood Initiative.

Hosley, C. A. and R. Montemayor. 1997. Fathers and adolescents. In M. E. Lamb, ed., *The role of the father in child development*, pp. 162–78. New York: John Wiley.

Jenny, C., T. A. Roesler, and K. L. Poyer. 1994. Are children at risk for sexual abuse by homosexuals? *Pediatrics* 94(1): 41–44.

Kessler, B. 1997. Q&A: Texas foster parent and adoption policy. *Dallas Morning News,* November 11, p. 11.

Kids' Talk: A publication of Center Kids. 1999. www.gaycenter.org/kidstalk (October 12, 2000).

Kinsey, A. C., W. B. Pomeroy, and C. E. Martin. 1948. *Sexual behavior in the human male.* Philadelphia: W. B. Saunders.

Kirk, H. D. 1964. *Shared fate.* Glencoe, Ill.: Free Press.

Knibiehler, Y. 1995. Fathers, patriarchy, paternity. In M. C. P. van Dongen, G. A. B. Frinking, and M. J. G. Jacobs, eds., *Changing fatherhood: An interdisciplinary perspective*, pp. 201–14. Amsterdam: Thesis.

Koestner, R., C. Franz, and J. Weinberger. 1990. The family origins of empathic concern: A twenty-six-year longitudinal study. *Journal of Personality and Social Psychology* 58:709–17.

Lamb, M. E. 1997. The development of father-infant relationships. In M. E. Lamb, ed., *The role of the father in child development*, pp. 104–20. New York: John Wiley.

——., ed. 1986. *The father's role: Applied perspectives.* New York: John Wiley.

——. 1987. *The father's role: Cross cultural perspectives.* Hillsdale, N.J.: Erlbaum.

Lamb, M. E., J. H. Pleck, and J. A. Levine. 1985. The role of the father in child development: The effects of increased parental involvement. In B. B. Lahey and A. E. Kazdin, eds., *Advances in clinical child psychology*, 8:229–66. New York: Plenum.

Lancaster, K. 1996. *Keys to parenting an adopted child.* Hauppauge, N.Y.: Barron's.

Larson, R.and M. Richards. 1994. *Divergent lives: The emotional lives of mothers, fathers, and adolescents.* New York: Basic Books.

Lewis, C. 1997. Fathers and preschoolers. In M. E. Lamb, ed., *The role of the father in child development*, pp. 121–42. New York: John Wiley.

Lewis, M. and M. Weintraub. 1976. The father's role in the child's social network. In M. E. Lamb, ed., *The role of the father in child development*, pp. 157–84. New York: John Wiley.

Lutz, L. 2002. *Recruitment and retention of resource families: The promise and the paradox.* New York: National Resource Center for

Foster Care and Permanency Planning and Casey Family Programs.

Maas, H. S. and R. E. Engler. 1959. *Children in need of parents.* New York: Columbia University Press.

Mallon, G. P. 1998a. Knowledge for practice with gay and lesbian persons. In G. P. Mallon, ed., *Foundations of social work practice with gay and lesbian person,* pp. 1–30. New York: Haworth.

———. 1998b. Social work practice with gay and lesbian persons within families. In G. P. Mallon, ed., *Foundations of social work practice with gay and lesbian persons,* pp. 145–81. New York: Haworth.

———. 1999. *Let's get this straight: A gay and lesbian–affirming approach to child welfare.* New York: Columbia University Press.

———. 2000. Gay men and lesbians as adoptive parents. *Journal of Gay and Lesbian Social Services* 11(4): 1–21.

Maluccio, A. N., E. Fein, and K. A. Olmstead. 1986. *Permanency planning for children: Concepts and methods.* New York: Tavistock.

Marcia, J. E. 1980. Identity in adolescence. In J. Adelson, ed., *Handbook of adolescent psychiatry,* pp. 159–87. New York: John Wiley.

Marindin, H. 1997. *The handbook for single adoptive parents.* Chevy Chase, Md.: Committee for Single Parents.

Markowitz, L. 2002. Queer generations: Talking to Terry Boggis about the Gayby boom. *In the Family* 7, no. 4 (spring): 14–16, 26.

Martin. A. 1993. *The lesbian and gay parenting handbook: Creating and raising our families.* New York: HarperPerennial.

McFarland, E. 1998. Foster care ban still sought for gays but not singles. *Arkansas Democratic Gazette,* August 26, p. 1B.

McPherson, D. 1993. Gay parenting couples: Parenting arrangements, arrangement satisfaction, and relationship satisfaction. Ph.D. diss. Pacific Graduate School of Psychology, Palo Alto, Calif.

McRoy, R. and L. Zurcher. 1983. *Transracial adoptees: The adolescent years.* Springfield, Ill.: Charles C. Thomas.

McRoy, R. G., Z. Oglesby, and H. Grape. 1997. Achieving same-race adoptive placements for African American children: Culturally sensitive practice approaches. *Child Welfare* 76(1): 85–104.

Melina, L. R. 1998. *Raising adopted children.* New York: Quill.

Miles, M. A. Huberman. 1984. *Qualitative data analysis.* Beverly Hills, Calif.: Sage.

Miller, B. 1979. Gay fathers and their children. *Family Coordinator* 28:544–52.

Mitchell, V. 1996. Two moms: Contribution of the planned lesbian family and the deconstruction of gendered parenting. In J. Laird and R.-J. Green, eds., *Lesbians and gays in couples and families: A handbook for therapists*, pp. 343–57. San Francisco: Jossey-Bass.

Mizrahi, T. and J. S. Abramson. 1994. Collaboration between social workers and physicians: An emerging typology. In E. Sherman and W. Reid, eds., *Qualitative research in social work*, pp. 135–51. New York: Columbia University Press.

Moseley, J. and E. Thompson. 1995. Fathering behavior and child outcomes: The role of race and poverty. In W. Marsiglio, ed., *Fatherhood contemporary theory, research, and social policy*, pp. 148–65. Thousand Oaks, Calif.: Sage.

Muzio, C. 1993. Lesbian co-parenting: On being the invisible (m)other. *Smith College Studies in Social Work* 63(3): 215–29.

———. 1996. Lesbians choosing children: Creating families, creating narratives. In J. Laird and R.-J. Green, eds., *Lesbians and gays in couples and families: A handbook for therapists*, pp. 358–69. San Francisco: Jossey-Bass.

National Adoption Information Clearinghouse. April 2000. *Gay and lesbian adoptive parents: Resources for professionals and parents.* www. calib.com/naic/pubs/f_gay.cfm (April 2, 2003).

Nelson, N. 1997. *When gay and lesbian people adopt.* Seattle, Wash.: Northwest Adoption Exchange.

Newton, D. E. 1978. Homosexual behavior and child molestation: A review of the evidence. *Adolescence* 13:205–15.

North American Council on Adoptable Children. 2002. *Policy statement on gay and lesbian foster and adoptive parenting.* St. Paul, Minn.: North American Council on Adoptable Children.

Offer, D. 1969. *The psychological world of the teenager: A study of normal adolescence.* New York: Basic Books.

Opie, A. 1992. Qualitative research appropriation of the "other" and empowerment. *Feminist Review* 40:52–69.

O'Reilly, B. 2002. Rosie O' Donnell. *New York Blade*, April 5, p. 14.

Patterson, C. J. 1994. Lesbian and gay couples considering parenthood: An agenda for research, service, and advocacy. In L. A. Kurdek, ed., *Social services for gay and lesbian couples*, pp. 33–56. New York: Harrington Park Press.

———. 1995. Lesbian mothers, gay fathers, and their children. In A. R. D'Augelli and C. J. Patterson, eds., *Gay, lesbian, and bisexual identities over the lifespan*, pp. 262–92. Oxford: Oxford University Press.

————. 1996. Lesbian mothers and their children: Findings from the Bay Area families study. In J. Laird and R.-J. Green, eds., *Lesbians and gays in couples and families: A handbook for therapists,* pp. 420–38. San Francisco: Jossey-Bass.

Patterson, C. J., and R. W. Chan. 1997. Gay fathers. In M. E. Lamb, ed., *The role of the father in child development,* pp. 245–60. New York: John Wiley.

Pavao, J. M. 1998. *The family of adoption.* Boston: Beacon.

Pelton, L. H. 1991. Beyond permanency planning: Restructuring the public child welfare system. *Social Work* 36(4): 337–44.

Pharr, S. 1988. *Homophobia: A weapon of sexism.* Little Rock, Ark.: Chardon Press.

Pierce, W. 1992. Adoption and other permanency considerations. *Children and Youth Services Review* 14(1/2): 61–66.

Pies, C. 1985. *Considering parenthood: A workbook for lesbians.* San Francisco: Spinsters/Aunt Lute.

————. 1990. Lesbians and the choice to parent. In F. W. Bozett and M. B. Sussman, eds., *Homosexuality and family relations,* pp. 138–50. New York: Harrington Park Press.

Pleck, J. H. 1982. *Husbands' and wives' paid work, family work, and adjustment.* Wellesley, Mass.: Wellesley College Center for Research on Women.

Pollack, J. S. 1995. *Lesbian and gay families: Redefining parenting in America.* New York: Franklin Watts.

Popenoe, D. 1989. The family transformed. *Family Affairs* 2(2/3): 1–5.

————. 1996. *Life without father.* New York: Free Press.

Radian, N. 1994. Primary caregiving father in intact families. In A. E. Gottfried and A. W. Gottfried, eds., *Redefining families: Implications for children's development,* pp. 11–54. New York: Plenum.

Reid, W. 1994. Reframing the epistemological debate. In E. Sherman and W. Reid, eds., *Qualitative research in social work,* pp. 464–81. New York: Columbia University Press.

Ricketts, W. 1991. *Lesbian and gay men as foster parents.* Portland, Minn.: National Resource center for Management and Administration.

Ricketts, W. and R. A. Achtenberg. 1990. Adoption and foster parenting for lesbians and gay men: Creating new traditions in family. In F. W. Bozett and M. B. Sussman, eds., *Homosexuality and family relations,* pp. 83–118. Binghamton, N.Y.: Harrington Park Press.

Riley, C. 1988. American kinship: A lesbian account. *Feminist Issues* 8:75–94.

Roberston, L. 1996. All clear over surrogate baby. *Glasgow (Scotland) Herald,* September 3, p. 1.

Rothman, B. 1996. Lesbian motherhood—before it was fashionable. *In the Family* 2, no. 1 (fall): 20.

Saghir, M. T. and E. Robins. 1973. *Male and female homosexuality: A comprehensive investigation.* Baltimore, Md.: Williams and Wilkins.

Savage, D. 1999. *The kid (What happened after my boyfriend and I decided to go get pregnant).* New York: Dutton.

Sbordone, A. J. 1993. Gay men choosing fatherhood. Ph.D. diss. Department of Psychology, City University of New York.

Schon, D. A. 1995. Reflective inquiry in social work practice. In P. McCartt-Hess and E. J. Mullen, eds., *Practitioner-researcher partnerships: Building knowledge from, in, and for practice,* pp. 31–55. Washington, D.C.: National Association of Social Workers.

Seidel, J. V., R. Kjolseth, and E. Seymour, E. 1988. The Ethnograph. Version 3.0. Software for qualitative analysis. Corvallis, Ore.: Qualis Research Associates.

Shernoff, M. 1996. Gay men choosing to be fathers. In M. Shernoff, ed., *Human services for gay people: Clinical and community practice,* pp. 41–54. New York: Haworth.

Shireman, J. and P. Johnson. 1976. Single persons as adoptive parents. *Social Service Review* 50(1): 103–16.

Strah, D. and K. Timken (2003). *Gay Dads: A Celebration of Fatherhood.* New York: J. P. Tarcher.

St. Pierre, T. 1999. *Gay and lesbian adoption: State of the issue.* Washington, D.C.: Human Rights Campaign.

———. 1985. Single parent adoptions: A longitudinal study. *Children and Youth Service Review* 7(4): 321–34.

Smothers, R. 1997a. Court lets two gay men jointly adopt child. *New York Times,* October 23, p. B5.

———. 1997b. Accord lets gay couples adopt jointly. *New York Times,* December 18, p. B4.

Solot, D. 1998. *Guidelines for adoption workers: Writing lesbian, gay, bisexual, and transgender homestudies for special needs adoptions.* Springfield, Va.: Adoption Resource Exchange for Single Parents.

Strauss, A. 1987. *Qualitative analysis for social scientists.* Cambridge: Cambridge University Press.

Strauss, A. L. and J. Corbin. 1990. *Basics of qualitative research: Grounded theory procedure and techniques.* Newbury Park, Calif.: Sage.

———. 1998. *The basics of qualitative research: Techniques and procedures*

for developing grounded theory. 2d ed. Thousand Oaks, Calif.:
 Sage.
Sullivan, A., ed. 1995. *Issues in gay and lesbian adoption: Proceedings of the
 Fourth Annual Pierce-Warwick Adoption Symposium.* Washington,
 D.C.: Child Welfare League of America.
Szymanski, K. 1997. New Jersey couples win adoption rights. *New York
 Blade,* December 19, p. A1.
Tanner, A. 1996. Minister says foster children belong with "natural"
 families. *Edmonton (Canada) Journal,* August 16, p. 2.
Tasker, F. L. and S. Golombok. 1997. *Growing up in a lesbian family:
 Effects on child development.* New York: Guilford.
Taylor, N. 1994. Gay and lesbian youth: Challenging the policy of
 denial. In T. De Crescenzo, ed., *Helping gay and lesbian youth:
 New policies, new programs, new practices,* pp. 39–73. New York:
 Haworth.
Testa, M. and N. Rolock. 1999. Professional foster care: A future
 worth pursuing? *Child Welfare* 78:108–24.
Triseliotis, J., J. Shireman, and M. Hundleby. 1997. *Adoption: Theory,
 policy and practice.* London: Cassell.
Tuchman, B. W. 1979. In search of history. *Radcliffe Quarterly* 15(1):
 33–37.
Turner, C. S. 1999. *Adoption journeys: Parents tell their stories.* Ithaca,
 N.Y.: McBooks Press.
van Dongen, M. 1995. Men's aspirations concerning child care: The
 extent to which they are realized. In M. C. P. van Dongen, G.
 A. B. Frinking, and M. J. G. Jacobs eds., *Changing fatherhood:
 An interdisciplinary perspective,* pp. 91–105. Amsterdam: Thesis.
Verhovek, S. H. 1997. Homosexual foster parent sets off a debate in
 Texas. *New York Times,* November 30, p. A20.
Weiss, J. S. 1998. *Your second child.* New York: Basic Books.
Weston, K. 1991. *Families we choose: Gay and lesbian kinship.* New
 York: Columbia University Press.
Williams, M. 1997. Texas state employee challenges lesbian foster
 parents. *Athens (Texas) Daily News,* December 24, p. 1.
Wolf, A. E. 2002. *Get out of my life: The parent's guide to the new teenager.*
 New York: Farrar, Straus and Giroux.
Yankelovitch, D. 1974. The meaning of work. In J. Rosow, ed., *The
 worker and the job.* Englewood Cliffs, N.J.: Prentice-Hall.

Index

adolescence: new issues in, 103, 104; pain of being different, 99–100, 102–105, 145

adoption, 5–7, 18, 45–58; antigay adoption bans, 9; antigay bias of child welfare system, 39, 43–44, 139–147; application process, 53; assessment of future parents, 54–56, 144; broader range of potential parents, 18; changes and stresses, 66–78; comments and questions of others about, 127, 129–130; cultural differences, 117–120; defined, 45; demographics and, 141; evaluation by social worker, 54; finalization, 95–96; foster care as precursor of, 37–38, 45, 46, 48; home study, 54–56; homecoming, 59–61; independent adoption, 52; initial impact of, 59–66; insensitive remarks of others, 127–128, 129–130; international adoptions, 50–51; modern view of, 140; openness about sexual orientation, 54–55, 145; policy of inclusiveness, 17–19; private adoptions, 49–50; process, 24, 52–58; public

adoptions, 48–49; racial issues, 117–120; search for birth families, 99, 101–102; second-parent adoptions, 7, 8, 145; stability of parental relationship, 13–14; starting the process, 46–52; state legal response to, 7–9, 145; statistics, 6; telling children about, 96–97, 98; training for, 52–54; transracial adoption, 117–120, by unmarried couples, 8. *See also* family formation

Adoption and Safe Families Act (ASFA), 5–6, 17–18, 37, 45–46, 140

Adoption Resource Exchange for Single Parents, 143

Adoption Standards, of Child Welfare League of America (CWLA), 15

Adoptive Parents Coalition (APC), 31–32

AIDS, HIV-positive children, 27, 41–42, 62

Alaska, adoption by gay parents, 8

alternative insemination, 16

American Civil Liberties Union, Gay Rights Project, 8

antigay adoption bans, 9
antigay bias: attitudes and myths
about gays, 10–15; of child welfare
system, 39, 43–44, 139–147
APC. *See* Adoptive Parents Coalition
application process, adoption, 53
Arkansas: foster parenting by gays, 7,
9; gay and lesbian parenting, 9
"artificial" (alternative) insemination,
16
ASFA. *See* Adoption and Safe Families
Act

bias: of child welfare system, 139–147.
See also sexism
birth families: dynamics in, 23; search
for, 99, 101–102
birth parents: search for, 99, 101–102;
telling children about, 98
Boggis, Terry, 26–28, 41, 42, 71, 72,
84, 153

California, adoption by gay parents, 8
career: gay fatherhood and, 84–88;
men defined by work, 136
Center Kids, 25–27, 134–135
child rearing, women and, 23
child welfare agencies, gay and lesbian
parenting, 17–19; policy development by, 142–147
Child Welfare League of America
(CWLA), 13–14, 15 -16
child welfare system, 5, 6; attitudes and
biases of, 139–147; policy development, 142–147; sexism in, 134
children: challenges of having gay
parents, 96–105, 145; gender
socialization, 137–139; grieving for
lost family, 99, 100–101; health
insurance coverage for, 125; moral
well-being and gays, 11, 15; more
likely to be gay, 11, 14; myths
about gay men and, 10–11; pain of
being different, 99–100, 102–105,
145; pediatricians for, 123–124;
recreation issues, 125- 126; rejection by peers, 14; role models for,
11, 13, 138–139; school issues,

120–123; searching for birth
family, 99, 101–102; second child,
68–69, 80–82, 122–123; sexual
molestation of, 10, 12; sexual
orientation of, 14; social stigma
suffered by, 12, 14, 145; socialization of, 125–126, 137–139; study
subject demographics, 21; telling
about adoption, 96–98; telling
about birth families, 97; toys for,
137–138; wishing for a mom, 98–99
coming out, as gay dads, 108–111
communication, 75–76, 78–80;
coming out as gay dad, 108–111;
openness about sexual orientation,
54–55; telling children about
adoption, 96–98; telling children
about birth families, 97
community response, 69–71,
108–131; coming out as gay dad,
108–111; hostile male neighbors,
115–116; neighbors, 113–116;
questions about missing mother,
129–130; single dads, 116
community support, for gay
fatherhood, 65–66
Connecticut, adoption by gay parents, 8
constant comparative method, 151
coparents, separation of, 82–84
couple relationships: changes in after
adoption, 75–76; separation of
coparents, 82–84; stable and
committed, 13, 144
creating family. *See* family formation
cultural differences, adoption,
117–120
CWLA. *See* Child Welfare League of
America

dating, by single parents, 75
demographics, adoption and, 141
division of labor, 136–137
doctors for children, gay fathers and,
123–124
"don't ask, don't tell" attitude, 141

family: father's role in, 135; gender
roles in, 136–139

family formation, 47, 59–105; changes
and stresses, 66–78; finalization of
adoption, 95–96; homecoming, 59–
61; overcompensation, 71–74
family-of-origin reactions, gay
fatherhood, 93–95
"family values" ideology, 9
fatherhood: desire for in gay men,
28–33; expanding definitions of,
135–136; realities of day-to-day
parenting, 66–71, 111–113;
research in heterosexual context, 3;
stereotypes, 23; See also gay fatherhood; lesbian parenting; parenthood
finalization, of adoption, 95–96
Florida, adoption by gay parents, 8, 9
formal kinship care, 35
foster care, 5–7, 18, 36–45; adoption
following, 37–38, 45, 46, 48; antigay bias, 39, 43–44; formal kinship
care, 35; principal goal, 45; pro-
fessionalizing, 44–45; state legal
response to, 7; statistics, 6; training
for gay men about role, 42–43
friends, loss of after adoption, 88–93

Gay and Lesbian Parenting Coalition,
25
gay community: reframing role in,
128–129; relationship of gay fathers
to, 88–93, 108–131
gay couple: changes in relationship
after adoption, 75–76; communication and negotiation, 75–76, 78–
80; dividing roles and duties, 76–
77; separation of, 82–84; stable
committed relationships, 13, 144
gay fatherhood: career issues, 84–88;
changes and stresses, 66–78;
changes in couple's relationship,
75–76; children more likely to be
gay, 11, 14; choosing, 3–5, 135–
136, 145- 146; coming out as gay
dad, 108–111; comments and questions of others, 127, 129–130; communication, 75–76, 78–80; community reaction, 69–71, 108–131;
community support, 65–66; desire

to become a father, 28–33; dividing
roles and duties, 76–77; emotional
adjustment to, 66–71; family-of-
origin reactions, 93–95; feelings of
inadequacy, 63–64; "friend" to help
raise children, 16–17; gender
politics and, 131–147; health care
providers and, 123–124; health
insurance coverage, 125; history,
27–28; of HIV-positive children,
27, 41–42, 62; homecoming,
59–61; initial impact of, 59–66;
insensitive remarks of others, 127–
128, 128–130; juggling work and
family, 85–86; by kinship/relative
care, 33–36; loss of long-time
friends, 88–93; myths about effect
of on children, 11; neighbors and,
113–116; nonlegal parents, 77–78;
openness about sexual orientation,
54–55, 145; overcompensation, 71–
74; pathways to, 33–42; pioneers,
24–28; race and cultural issues,
117–120; realities of day-to-day
parenting, 66–71, 111–113;
recreation issues, 125–126; research
study for present book, 19–22,
149 158; school issues, 120–123;
second child, 68–69, 80–82, 122–
123; separation of coparents, 82–84;
sexism and parenthood, 132 139;
single dads, 17, 74–75, 116; social
stigma suffered by child, 12, 14,
145; social validation for assuming
traditionally female role, 137–139;
stability of parental relationship,
13–14; statistics, 3–4; telling
children about adoption, 96–98;
telling children about birth
families, 97; women's reaction to,
69–70, 138. See also adoption; foster
care
gay fathers, 3–4; coming out as gay
dads, 108–111; interviews with,
19–21, 151–153; loss of long-time
friends, 88–93; overcompensation,
71–74; reframing role in gay
community, 128; relationship to

gay community, 88–93, 108–131;
separation of coparents, 82–84
gay men: antigay attitudes and myths,
10–15; changes in couple's
relationship after adoption, 75-
76; choosing gay fatherhood, 3–5,
135–136, 145–146; desire to
become a father, 28–33, 145;
internalized sexism, 133; myths
about, 10–15; pedophilia by, 12; as
primary caregivers, 24; relationship
to gay fathers, 88–93; separation of
coparents, 82–84; social validation
for assuming traditionally female
role, 137–139; stable committed
relationships, 13, 144; *See also* gay
community; gay couple; gay
fatherhood; gay fathers
Gay Rights Project (ACLU), 8
gender politics, gay fatherhood and,
131–147
gender roles: in family, 136–139;
internalized homophobia and sexism,
133; research on fatherhood and, 3;
single parent, 17; socialization for,
137–139
gender socialization, 137–139
Georgia, gay and lesbian parenting, 9
grounded theory, 149–151

harassment, of children of gay parents,
12, 14
health care providers, gay fathers and,
123–124
heterocentrism, 4, 4n
HIV-positive children, 27, 41–42, 62
home study, adoption, 54–56
homecoming, adoption, 59–61
homophobia, internalized, 133
homosexuality: "don't ask, don't tell"
attitude, 141; myths about, 10–15;
same-gender marriage, 8; stable
committed relationships, 13, 144;
See also gay man; lesbians

Idaho, gay and lesbian parenting, 9
Illinois, adoption by gay parents, 8
independent adoption, 52

Indiana: foster parenting by gays, 7, 9;
gay and lesbian parenting, 9
informal kinship care, 35
internalized sexism, 133
international adoptions, 50–51

kinship care, 33–36
Kirk, H. David, 97–98

Lavender Moms, 25
lesbian parenting, 10; children more
likely to be lesbian, 14; history, 25;
role models for boys, 139
lesbians: antigay attitudes and myths,
separation of coparents, 82–84;
stable committed relationships, 13,
144; *See also* lesbian parenting
LGBT Community Center, 25

MAPP training, 52–54
Massachusetts, adoption by gay
parents, 8
men: defined by work, 136; internalized sexism and homophobia, 133;
patriarchial roles for, 136–137
Mississippi, adoption by gay parents, 8
moral well-being, of children, 11, 15
mothers: child rearing by, 23; children
wishing for, 98–99; gay fathers'
camaraderie with, 128- 129; lack of,
98; questions about lack of, 129–130
multiple-partner parenting, 25

National Adoption Information
Clearinghouse, 143
Nebraska, foster parenting by gays, 7,
9
negotiation, 75–76, 78–80
neighbors, gay fathers and, 113–116
New Hampshire, fostering parenting
by gays, 9
New Jersey, adoption by gay parents,
7, 8, 145
New York, adoption by gay parents,
8
New York State Council on Adoptable
Children (NYSCAC), 31
nonlegal parents, 77–78

North American Council on Adoptable
Children, 14
NYSCAC. See New York State Council
on Adoptable Children

O'Donnell, Rosie, 9
Ohio, adoption by gay parents, 7–8
Oklahoma, gay and lesbian parenting,
9
openness: about being gay dad,
108–111; about sexual orientation,
54–55, 145
out-of-home care. See adoption; foster
care
overcompensation, by gay fathers,
71–74

parenthood, 16; expanding definitions
of, 135–136; impulse to parent, 11;
mommy-driven nature of, 69–71;
multiple-partner parenting, 25;
nonlegal parents, 77–78; realities of
day-to-day parenting, 66–71, 111–
113; sexism and, 132–139; transition to, 3–5; See also fatherhood; gay
fatherhood; lesbian parenting
pediatricians, gay fathers and, 123–124
pedophilia, 10, 12
play dates, 125–126
Pop Luck, 135
Pride Training, 53
private adoptions, 49–50
public adoptions, 48–49

race, transracial adoption, 117–120
racism, 120
recreation, for children, 125–126
rejection by peers, children of gay
parents, 12, 14
relative care, 33–36
research study (for present book),
19–22, 149–158; characteristics of
children, 21; data analysis, 154–
156; data collection methods, 151;
grounded theory, 149–151, 154,
155; interviewees, 19–22, 151–153
responsibilities, redefining after
adoption, 76–77

role models, for children, 11, 13, 138–
139
roles: division of labor, 136–137;
expanding definitions of fatherhood,
135–136; father's role in family,
135–139; gender socialization, 137–
139; patriarchal roles, 136–137;
redefining after adoption, 76–77

same-gender couples: adoption by, 8;
marriage, 8–9; parenthood. See gay
fatherhood; lesbian parenting
same-gender partner adoptions, 7, 8,
145
school issues, gay fatherhood, 120–
123
second child, 68–69, 80–82, 122–123
second-parent adoptions, 7, 8, 145
separation, of coparents, 82–84
sexism: in child welfare system, 134;
definitions of parenthood, 135–136;
internalized, 133; parenthood and,
132–139; patriarchal roles for men,
136–137; social validation for
assuming traditionally female role,
137–139; voice and choice, 133–
135; See also bias
sexual molestation, of children, 10,
12
sexual orientation: of children, 14;
"don't ask, don't tell" attitude, 141;
openness about, 54–55, 145
single dads, 17, 74–75; community
response to, 116; dating by, 75
social stigma, to child, 12, 14, 145
social worker, evaluation by for
adoption, 54
socialization, of children, 125–126
South Carolina: foster parenting by
gays, 7, 9; gay and lesbian
parenting, 9
South Dakota, gay and lesbian
parenting, 9
states, adoption law in, 7–9, 145
stereotypes: antiadoption attitudes, 9;
fatherhood, 23
stigma, suffered by children, 12, 14,
145

Texas, gay and lesbian parenting, 9

training: for adoption, 52–54; for foster care, 42–43

transracial adoption, 117–120

unmarried couples, adoption by, 8

Utah, adoption by gay parents, 8

Vermont, adoption by gay parents, 8

Washington, D.C., adoption by gay parents, 8

Washington state, adoption by gay parents, 8

women: child rearing by, 23; gay fathers' camaraderie with, 128–129; reaction to sole male parent, 69–71, 138

work: career issues and gay fatherhood, 84–88; family work, 137; men defined by, 136

About the Author

Gerald P. Mallon, DSW, is associate professor and executive director of the National Resource Center for Foster Care and Permanency Planning at Hunter College School of Social Work in New York City. His research interests focus on the experiences of gay and lesbian children, youth, and families within the context of child welfare policy, practice, and service delivery. Mallon is the author of *We Don't Exactly Get the Welcome Wagon: The Experiences of Gay and Lesbian Adolescents in Child Welfare Systems* (Columbia University Press, 1998), *Let's Get This Straight: A Gay and Lesbian–Affirming Approach to Child Welfare Systems* (Columbia University Press, 1999), *Working with Lesbian and Gay Youth: A Youth Worker's Perspective* (Child Welfare League of America Press, 2001), and *Facilitating Permanency for Older Adolescents: A Toolbox for Youth Permanency* (Child Welfare League of America Press, 2003); editor of *Foundations of Social Work Practice with Gay and Lesbian Persons* (Haworth, 1998) and *Social Services for Transgendered Persons* (Haworth, 1999); and coeditor of *Contemporary Issues in Permanency Planning* (Child Welfare League of America Press, 2002).

Mallon, his partner, and their children live in New York City and New Orleans.

Correspondence may be sent to 129 East 79th Street, Suite 801, New York, New York 10021 or via e-mail at mrengmal aol.com.